Dawn Atkins, MA
Editor

Lesbian Sex Scandals: Sexual Practices, Identities, and Politics

Lesbian Sex Scandals: Sexual Practices, Identities, and Politics has been co-published simultaneously as *Journal of Lesbian Studies,* Volume 3, Number 3 1999.

Pre-publication
REVIEWS,
COMMENTARIES,
EVALUATIONS . . .

"**G**rounded in material practices, this collection explores confrontation and coincidence among identity politics, 'scandalous' sexual practices, and queer theory and feminism. . . . It expands notions of lesbian identification and lesbian community."

Maria Pramaggione, PhD
Assistant Professor, Film Studies
North Carolina State University
Raleigh

D1732906

Lesbian Sex Scandals: Sexual Practices, Identities, and Politics

Lesbian Sex Scandals: Sexual Practices, Identities, and Politics has been co-published simultaneously as *Journal of Lesbian Studies,* Volume 3, Number 3 1999.

Lesbian Sex Scandals: Sexual Practices, Identities, and Politics

Dawn Atkins, MA
Editor

Lesbian Sex Scandals: Sexual Practices, Identities, and Politics, edited by Dawn Atkins, was simultaneously issued by The Haworth Press, Inc., under the same title, as a special issue of *Journal of Lesbian Studies,* Volume 3, Number 3 1999, Esther D. Rothblum, Editor.

Harrington Park Press
An Imprint of
The Haworth Press, Inc.
New York • London

ISBN 1-56023-118-1

Published by

Harrington Park Press, 10 Alice Street, Binghamton, NY 13904-1580 USA

Harrington Park Press is an imprint of The Haworth Press, Inc., 10 Alice Street, Binghamton, Ny 13904-1580 USA.

Lesbian Sex Scandals: Sexual Practices, Identities, and Politics has been co-published simultaneously as *Journal of Lesbian Studies* ™, Volume 3, Number 3 1999.

The development, preparation, and publication of this work has been undertaken with great care. However, the publisher, employees, editors, and agents of The Haworth Press and all imprints of The Haworth Press, Inc., including The Haworth Medical Press® and Pharmaceutical Products Press®, are not responsible for any errors contained herein or for consequences that may ensue from use of materials or information contained in this work. Opinions expressed by the author(s) are not necessarily those of The Haworth Press, Inc.

Library of Congress Cataloging-in-Publication Data

Lesbian sex scandals : sexual practices, identities, and politics / Dawn Atkins, editor.
     p. cm.
     "Has been co-published simultaneously as Journal of lesbian studies, Volume 3, Number 3, 1999."
     Includes bibliographical references and index.
     ISBN 0-7890-0548-4 (alk. paper)–ISBN 1-56023-118-1 (pbk. alk. paper)
     1. Lesbians–United States–Identity. 2. Lesbians–United States–Sexual behavior. 3. Lesbians–United States–Political Activity. I. Atkins, Dawn. II. Journal of lesbian studies.
HQ75.6.U6L393 1998
306.76'63–dc21
                                       98-34517
                                          CIP

INDEXING & ABSTRACTING

Contributions to this publication are selectively indexed or abstracted in print, electronic, online, or CD-ROM version(s) of the reference tools and information services listed below. This list is current as of the copyright date of this publication. See the end of this section for additional notes.

- *Abstracts in Social Gerontology: Current Literature on Aging,* National Council on the Aging, Library, 409 Third Street SW, 2nd Floor, Washington, DC 20024

- *CNPIEC Reference Guide: Chinese National Directory of Foreign Periodicals*, P.O. Box 88, Beijing, People's Republic of China

- *Contemporary Women's Issues,* Responsive Databases Services, 23611 Chagrin Boulevard, Suite 320, Beachwood, OH 44122

- *Feminist Periodicals: A Current Listing of Contents,* Women's Studies Librarian-at-Large, 728 State Street, 430 Memorial Library, Madison, WI 53706

- *Gay & Lesbian Abstracts,* National Information Services Corporation, 306 East Baltimore Pike, 2nd Floor, Media, PA 19063

- *HOMODOK/"Relevant" Bibliographic database, Documentation Centre for Gay & Lesbian Studies, University of Amsterdam (selective printed abstracts in "Homologie" and bibliographic computer databases covering cultural, historical, social and political aspects of gay & lesbian topics)*, HOMODOK-ILGA Archive, O.Z. Achterburgwal 185, NL-1012 DK Amsterdam, The Netherlands

- *Index to Periodical Articles Related to Law,* University of Texas, 727 East 26th Street, Austin, TX 78705

(continued)

- *INTERNET ACCESS (& additional networks) Bulletin Board for Libraries ("BUBL") coverage of information resources on INTERNET, JANET, and other networks.*
  - <URL:http://bubl.ac.uk/>
  - The new locations will be found under <URL:http://bubl.ac.uk.link/>.
  - Any existing BUBL users who have problems finding information on the new service should contact the BUBL help line by sending e-mail to <bubl@bubl.ac.uk>.
  The Andersonian Library, Curran Building, 101 St. James Road, Glasgow G4 0NS, Scotland

- *Public Affairs Information Bulletin (PAIS),* Public Affairs Information Service, Inc., 521 West 43rd Street, New York, NY 10036-4396

- *Referativnyi Zhurnal (Abstracts Journal of the All-Russian Institute of Scientific and Technical Information),* 20 Usievich Street, Moscow 125219, Russia

- *Sociological Abstracts (SA),* Sociological Abstracts, Inc., P.O. Box 22206, San Diego, CA 92192-0206

- *Studies on Women Abstracts,* Carfax Publishing Company, P. O. Box 25, Abingdon, Oxon OX14 3UE United Kingdom

- *Women "R" CD/ROM. A new full text Windows Database on CD/ROM. Presents full depth coverage of the wide range of subjects that impact and reflect the lives of women. Can be reached at 1 (800) 524-7922, www.slinfo.com, or e-mail: hoch@slinfo.com,* Softline Information, Inc., 20 Summer Street, Stamford, CT 06901

- *Women's Studies Index (indexed comprehensively),* G.K. Hall & Co., P. O. Box 159, Thorndike, ME 04986

(continued)

SPECIAL BIBLIOGRAPHIC NOTES

related to special journal issues (separates)
and indexing/abstracting

- [ ] indexing/abstracting services in this list will also cover material in any "separate" that is co-published simultaneously with Haworth's special thematic journal issue or DocuSerial. Indexing/abstracting usually covers material at the article/chapter level.

- [ ] monographic co-editions are intended for either non-subscribers or libraries which intend to purchase a second copy for their circulating collections.

- [ ] monographic co-editions are reported to all jobbers/wholesalers/approval plans. The source journal is listed as the "series" to assist the prevention of duplicate purchasing in the same manner utilized for books-in-series.

- [ ] to facilitate user/access services all indexing/abstracting services are encouraged to utilize the co-indexing entry note indicated at the bottom of the first page of each article/chapter/contribution.

- [ ] this is intended to assist a library user of any reference tool (whether print, electronic, online, or CD-ROM) to locate the monographic version if the library has purchased this version but not a subscription to the source journal.

- [ ] individual articles/chapters in any Haworth publication are also available through the Haworth Document Delivery Service (HDDS).

ABOUT THE EDITOR

Dawn Atkins, MA, is a nationally known writer, speaker, and editor. She has a Masters in and is currently a PhD candidate in Anthropology at the University of Iowa. She is editor of several collections, including *Looking Queer: Body Image and Identity in Lesbian, Bisexual, Gay, and Transgender Communities* (The Haworth Press, Inc., 1998), as well as special issues of *Journal of Homosexuality,* on gay identity and sexual practices, and *Journal of Lesbian, Gay and Bisexual Identity,* on being queer and disabled. She has done ethnographic studies of lesbian, gay, and bisexual perspectives of the body in Iowa City, Iowa, and with transgendered/transsexual people in both San Francisco and Amsterdam.

CONTENTS

Acknowledgments

This collection owes its start to the energetic and sometimes heated discussions provided by the organizers and participants of the Lavender Languages and Linguistics Conference at American University. In particular, I would like to thank William Leap for encouraging John Heyworth and me to organize a panel on questions of sexual practices and identities. Some of these papers and early portions of the introduction were presented on September 20, 1997 at "Talking Sex: Sexual Practices, Politics and Identities," at the 4th Annual Lavender Languages and Linguistics Conference. From there, further inspiration was provided by Esther Rothblum, who invited me to organize a special issue of *Journal of Lesbian Studies*.

I would also like to thank Florence Babb for her continued insights, guidance and encouragement. Wendy Chapkis, Ellen Lewin, Theo Van der Meer, and Gilbert Herdt have all provided important contributions to these ideas and supported my exploration of such controversial perspectives. Jill Nagle has my gratitude for her comments on an early draft of the introduction and her example as one who pushes the boundaries of inclusion.

And, as always, for the love and inspiration from the first woman of my heart, Mary Atkins.

Dawn Atkins

Introduction:
Lesbian Sex Scandals

Dawn Atkins

I mean the term *lesbian continuum* to include a range–through each woman's life and throughout history–of woman-identified experience, not simply the fact that a woman has had or consciously desired genital sexual experience with another woman.

–Rich 1986:51, originally 1980

"Lesbian" describes a relationship in which two women's strongest emotions and affections are directed toward each other. Sexual contact may be a part of the relationship to a greater or lesser degree, or it may be entirely absent. . . . But women who identify themselves as lesbian generally do not view lesbianism as a sexual phenomenon first and foremost.

–Faderman 1981:17-18,142

Dawn Atkins has an MA in Anthropology and is currently a PhD candidate at the University of Iowa. She is the editor of *Looking Queer: Body Image and Identity in Lesbian, Bisexual, Gay and Transgender Communities* (The Haworth Press, Inc., 1998). She has also guest edited a special issue of a forthcoming *Journal of Homosexuality.* Her area of specialty is the body and culture, especially with regards to sexuality, gender and identity. Her primary focus has been on the body image issues in the United States.

Address correspondence to: Dawn Atkins, Anthropology, 114 MacBride Hall, University of Iowa, Iowa City, IA 52242 (E-mail: dawn-atkins@uiowa.edu).

[Haworth co-indexing entry note]: "Introduction: Lesbian Sex Scandals." Atkins, Dawn. Co-published simultaneously in *Journal of Lesbian Studies* (The Haworth Press, Inc.) Vol. 3, No. 3, 1999, pp. 1-9; and: *Lesbian Sex Scandals: Sexual Practices, Identities, and Politics* (ed: Dawn Atkins) The Haworth Press, Inc., 1999, pp. 1-9; and: *Lesbian Sex Scandals: Sexual Practices, Identities, and Politics* (ed: Dawn Atkins) Harrington Park Press, an imprint of The Haworth Press, Inc., 1999, pp. 1-9. Single or multiple copies of this article are available for a fee from The Haworth Document Delivery Service [1-800-342-9678, 9:00 a.m. - 5:00 p.m. (EST). E-mail address: getinfo@haworthpressinc.com].

1

Lips pressed together, tongues touching, hands caressing and sweaty bodies–the glorious feeling of touching and being touched by a woman–lesbianism, I have been told, has nothing to do with this. It is primarily a political agenda. The test of a true feminist.

My mother taught me about feminism. Feminism was carrying signs in front of a building when the Junior Chamber of Commerce wouldn't admit girls. Feminism was writing papers about women for history classes. Feminism was marching in ERA demonstrations, even when men threw rocks at us. Feminism was being on call for the rape crisis hotline. Feminism's goal was equality for everyone. Feminism was my mother supporting and encouraging her four daughters to become strong and independent–and to change the world.

Jackie taught me something else. She taught me that being touched by another was what made it all worthwhile. She taught me the pleasure I could find in the arms of another female body. Feminism was the struggle and strength. Sex was a source of pleasure and comfort.

What of the transformative power of sexual experience? Despite isolation from other lesbigay people in 1970s small-town Oklahoma, I knew that I was *not straight*. Sexual experience was for me, as for many others, a defining moment in my identity. Although this is not true for everyone, we do ourselves, our lovers and our community, great disservice when we dismiss the power of sexual experience to shape our identities.

Did feminism influence my sexuality as well? Yes. My mother taught me feminism included fighting for the right to enjoy love and sex, with whomever I wanted–and that I should never give over the right to follow my own heart, mind or body. I think my radical feminist mother was unprepared for the directions her daughter would take these teachings. We are both feminist and she is proud of my work, but where sexual politics are concerned, we often take very different approaches.

This, in many ways, is the dilemma of this collection. The blending of feminism and lesbianism has led to as many contradictions and problems as it has solutions. While some lesbian theorists have articulated a view of lesbian that stands on feminist solidarity, others have felt that this approach has denied the history of a specifically lesbian sexuality (Nestle 1987, Califia 1994). And while having sex with a woman may not define who is a lesbian, certainly sexual practices have been at the heart of the controversies over who is *not* a lesbian. As the scholarship and personal histories of the contributors to this collection document, sexual practices are often at the core of lesbian sexual identities, communities and politics.

This collection grew out of a frustration with works in sexuality studies which seem to increasingly reify sexual identities and communities without regard to those "sweaty bodies." If sexual identity is so important—why does the reality of our sexual experiences seem to be irrelevant to so many of these discussions?

In *The Persistent Desire*, Parkin and Prosser also express that "language itself becomes the closet" (1992:44). And Jenny Corbett says:

> The very formality and aridity of academic language discourages subjectivity and self-disclosure. It might be seen, in this analysis that 'virtual' identity is the preserve of academic discourse whilst 'actual' identity is rejected as inappropriately raw. Language is important in that it forges a reality, a delineated discourse. If the 'actual' identity is submerged, it can find no voice. It becomes a non-reality. (1994:346)

I will point out here that I do not think that when academics aren't talking about sex, that means these sexual practices are any less real. (Or that academics don't have sex.) But I do think it impoverishes our theories of identity when their connection to actual sexual practices is lost. Lest you think I am over-reacting, I found it particularly humorous and frustrating that in the call for papers for this collection, more than half of the proposals did not mention sexual practices—this in spite of an explicit call for it.

Yet, I think there is more going on here than the difficulty of academics to ground their work in actual experience. I think that talking about sexual practices runs counter to many currents in the lesbian and gay rights movement. This movement has been quite successful in adopting a minority model for sexual orientation by emphasizing that gays are "just like everyone else" except for the gender of "who we love," that we are "born that way" and that, after all, "no one would choose to be gay." In her groundbreaking essay, "Epistemology of the Closet," Eve Sedgwick (1993) identified this as a "minoritizing" approach. This has been an effective way of arguing for inclusion—but only by downplaying sexual behavior. In this model "gay" is who we are, not what we do.

There are at least two stereotypes that this strategy attempts to counter. The first is the idea that homosexuality is "just about sex" and the second is the idea of contagion. The sexual stereotyping of homosexuality may be related to the "master status" of deviance (Thomson 1997:34), the idea that one characteristic defines the entire character of the person. To be sexually deviant is to be seen as overly and predominantly sexual. Yet, attempting to illustrate the breadth and humanity of homosexuals has been bought at the expense of desexualizing a sexual identity. We are not allowed to be both sexual and human. The idea of contagion and recruitment is still a popular homophobic theme. To nullify this fear, the gay rights movement has often relied on promoting acceptance based on the essential nature of gay identity, downplaying complicated sexual histories while at the same time recognizing that some homophobes may have "secret gay feelings." This strategy seems to rely on neutralizing the undercurrent fear that sexual orientation is more fluid, and therefore anyone may be "at risk" of becoming gay. If, on the other hand, gay identity is fixed and immutable, then one's own place in the hierarchy is assured. Heterosexuals need not fear becoming gay. If their children become gay, it is not their fault.

Unfortunately, although effective in promoting the rights of a sexual minority, these strategies rely on the stigmatization of homosexuality for their very persuasiveness. If one cannot and, more importantly, would not choose to be gay, then there is something inherently wrong with non-heterosexuality. The entire effect is one that reinforces binary oppositions of straight/gay, with heterosexual remaining the preferred category.

For lesbians, there may be additional problems to addressing sexual practices as well. First, the cultural conditioning of women in this culture to downplay sexuality. Second, the perceived need to distance themselves from what can be seen as overtly sexual behavior of gay men and the related stigmatization of AIDS. Also, what may have begun within lesbian feminism as an attempt to create space away from "patriarchy" has been transformed into what might now be seen as a way to make a place for lesbians within the very system many opposed. In recent years, the assimilationist lesbian and gay movement seems also be distancing itself from feminism as much as it is from sexuality. This move may leave lesbian feminists who are not interested in assimilation strategies in the position of needing to strengthen their claim on the definition of lesbian, lest they be erased in the new movement.

Given these strategies, it should not be too surprising that the inclusion of bisexuality and transsexualism people, let alone sadomasochism, polyamoury, butch/femme, and other radical sexual and gender practices have met with opposition from both lesbian and gay organizations focused on the "mainstreaming" of a lesbian/gay minority and lesbian feminists trying to hold onto the radical potential of their movement.

The inclusion of alternate sexual and gender identities and practices introduces fluidity that challenges the foundations the minority approach. Thomson argues that figures who defy classification into absolute categories "such as mulattos, freaks, transvestites, bisexuals, and other hybrids–elicit anxiety, hostility or pity and are always rigorously policed" (1997:34). For instance, bisexuality has the potential to upset the either/or of straight/gay and the reliance on the gender-object choice as the defining criteria for sexual desires and practices. Transgendered people challenge the very male/female dichotomy that these criteria are based on. Sadomasochism, butch/femme and polyamoury are just some of the contested sexual practices that have the potential to disrupt the careful narrative that says gays and lesbians are "just like straights," i.e., "normal," except for the gender of their partners.

It is of course, no coincidence that these alternative sexual and gender identities and practices are usually accepted as "queer." Queer, as a label and a theory, emphasizes a strategy of valorizing differences. Eve Sedgwick (1993) and Jeffrey Weeks (1985) have both pointed to queer theory as a break with the minority model, that pushes instead for inclusivity of difference and a more "universalizing" strategy. Weeks says the queer movement is "a challenge to rigid categorizations, by embracing all who would identify with the new politics, whatever their previous sexual histories, preferences, or activities" (1985:49).

It is also important to emphasize that the queer movement grew as much out of AIDS activism as it did from a rejection of identity politics. AIDS has forced researchers, activists–anyone interested in preventing AIDS–to look at sexual practices instead of assuming them from stated identities. What such research has overwhelmingly shown is that sexual practices are not accurately mapped by sexual categories or sexual identities. While the minority discourse may have been effective in fighting against job discrimination for many lesbians and gays, it did not help combat the spread of HIV. Only the examination of and destigmatization of sexual practices would have a chance of stopping the spread of HIV.

There are other consequences of reifying identities over sexual practices. First, the stigmatization of those sexual practices themselves and those who practice them. Second, the internalized self-hatred that comes with closeting. Third, creating divisions between people who could be working together. And fourth, the devaluing of differences that comes with assimilation strategies.

Some of us are not, and may not want to be, "just like everyone else." One high cost of the minoritizing approach is the loss of value for those who can't or won't fit the model. Although it would provide some protection for lesbians and gays who can assimilate, it still leaves many people outside the "norm." And to fit the norm, one must often erase the complexity of one's histories and desires. Witness the pain and anger experienced within lesbian communities when a lesbian-identified woman openly loves a man. The minoritizing approach is so reliant on the gay/straight dichotomy that it must reject her from the community and yet, unless she would erase her history, she will also be rejected by the straight community as well. Treatment of transgendered people illustrates the oppositional nature of this strategy which relies strongly on the immutability and separateness of male/female. Female to male transsexuals who identified as lesbians before transition are often seen as having betrayed the lesbian community. Male to female transsexuals who identify as lesbian are cast as infiltrators (Raymond 1979).

Also, the minority strategy is not always effective. Witness the German gay rights movement of the 1920s–although very successful at the time, the argument of the essential nature of gays and lesbians did not prevent the death of many at the hands of the Nazis, who also believed in the essential nature of this deviance and a eugenic approach to its eradication (Weeks 1985). More recently, Sedgwick points out how this separation of sexuality from identity resulted in the contradictory court decisions in which the Supreme Court ruled in Bowers vs. Hardwick that individual states were free to prohibit any acts they wish to define as "sodomy," without impinging any rights, and then shortly after the Ninth Circuit Court of Appeals ruled that homosexual persons are entitled to protection under the Equal Protection clause (1993:57). Apparently, since gay is who we are, not what we do, homosexual identity is protected, but homosexual sexual practices are not.

The problem remains though, how do groups intent on gaining acceptance and protection for lesbian, gay, and bisexual people achieve these gains without the successful minority strategy? And how do lesbian feminists retain the radical potential of their movement and the strength of their communities when the definitions of these identities and communities are being challenged from both without and within?

The authors in this collection address these and other issues of sexual practice and sexual politics. The combination of scholarship and experience reflected here focuses on the sweaty bodies that would claim or challenge lesbian identity and community. And although, like my mother and I, we will certainly not all agree on these issues, I believe these works address important experiences, questions and directions for anyone interested in lesbian sexuality.

Dana R. Shugar takes up the challenge of addressing the impact of queer theory on lesbian community, sexuality and identity. She addresses the problems of incorporating both theories and sexual practices which destabilize identity for a lesbian community that needs a stable base for socio-political activism. How will the lesbian community incorporate these queer elements in a way that strengthens rather than destroys?

Directly analyzing the mainstreaming of lesbian identity, Karen Yescavage and Jonathan Alexander take up the case of the first openly lesbian character on television, Ellen. By interrogating the presentation of identity in both the character, Ellen Morgan, and the actress/comedian who plays her, Ellen DeGeneres, they explore what is and, more importantly, is not said about lesbian sexuality and the meaning of lesbian identity. Is a lesbian a woman who sleeps with other women or a woman who does not sleep with men?

Hinda Seif's ethnographic work addresses this question through the personal narratives of three women who in some way identify as lesbian and are also attracted to men. Taking a direct look at one of the most controversial issues, Seif explores the way lesbian identification is more than gender attraction in the lives of some women, and how they negotiate this seeming contradiction.

Jumping in (with both feet) to explore some of the most heated arguments in lesbian feminism is Atara Stein with her analysis of the rejection of bisexuals, transsexuals and leatherwomen (S/M). Stein posits that these sexual and gender practices pose a challenge to binary thinking and the "lesbian purity test." She takes a lesbian and feminist stance supporting these practices and critiquing anti-S/M feminist arguments.

Teresa Hornsby combines feminist and religious studies training to argue for the ritual and radical potential of lesbian sadomasochism. She argues for the "socio/political power in the theater of SM" to subvert patriarchal "power games."

The reclaiming of women's history–particularly that of lesbians–has been an important feminist project. Nan Alamilla Boyd analyzes the way both "lesbian and transgender histories often recuperate the same historical figures" while at the same time giving them entirely different and sometimes opposing meanings. Here the importance of "birth bodies," sexuality and cross-gender behavior all provide for contradictions in the support of lesbian community and history.

Addressing another stigmatized practice/identity, Robin Maltz presents an argument for "stonebutch" and "stonefemme" subjectivity that rests on essentialized identities within highly sexualized practices. She further argues that neither lesbian feminist nor queer theory has been able to address the concerns of these issues and posit the need for a "dyke discourse" which would ground theory in female sexual subjectivity with attention to desire and sexual practice.

And while AIDS activism and research have brought an emphasis on gay male sexual practices, Christie Milliken's analysis of lesbian-produced safe-sex video tapes shows the way these mediums may also promote the visibility of lesbian sexual practices as well as promoting safe sex. She argues that there may be multiple purposes to the lesbian use of the normally gay male "pornographic vernacular" which also serve to counter the erasure of lesbian sexuality and community.

From down under, Myra J. Hird and Jenz Germon explore the "contradictions of authenticity as a defining feature of lesbian community in Aotearoa/New Zealand." They explore the way the marginalization of some sexual practices functions to help identify a "bounded community." They posit that while this has been "a strategic and useful political tool" it ultimately is in danger of "excluding and further fragmenting lesbian subjectivity."

Sally Abrahams brings us an "exploration of life-in-the-ghetto; twenty-five years of sex and politics, and wrestling with sexual correctness." Grounding her analysis in both her experience and the history of Australian lesbian community(ies), Abrahams chronicles the shifts and re-alignments of "ideology and practice" in lesbian sexuality.

Julie Inness addresses how a strategy of lesbian communities to distance themselves from "deviant" sexuality, particularly as embodied by gay male sexuality, has led to a limiting of sexual dialogue and fantasy among lesbians and the creation of a "potentially radical fringe of lesbian sexual outlaws."

Radical sex practices and identities are, according to Kathy Rudy, providing a new kind of sexual ethic based on community. Rudy looks at Western conceptions of sexual ethics based on monogamy and procreativity. She argues that when some lesbians and gays "want to assimilate into dominant culture," they do so by adopting and modifying these same ethics. Resistance to both the heterosexual and the lesbian/gay assimilationist models comes from groups who identify themselves as "sex radicals" who organize their lives on "a model that is fundamentally communal."

What this collection may show is that while the minority approach has its benefits and may even be an important strategy in some situations, it may ultimately be self-defeating. By neutralizing the fear of contagion, downplaying the fluidity and changeability of sexual desires and identity, minority models may also neutralize the power to challenge the hierarchy of sexuality and gender systems and further fracture lesbian communities at a time when inclusion might be more powerful and effective. What if we championed the diversity of sexuality, pleasure, and desire as a core value? If we adopt a "universalizing" (Sedgwick 1993) approach that emphasizes the importance of sexual freedom across a spectrum of identity, we have a larger and stronger community base to challenge oppression. This was my naive interpretation of my sexual experience and feminist idealism over twenty years ago, and one, in spite of all the challenges it poses, I still believe is crucial to all our futures.

REFERENCES

Califia, Pat. *Public Sex: The Culture of Radical Sex*. Pittsburgh: Cleis Press, 1994.

Corbett, Jenny. "A Proud Label: Exploring the Relationship Between Disability Politics and Gay Pride." *Disability & Society* 9(3):343-357, 1994.

Faderman, Lillian. *Surpassing the Love of Men: Romantic Friendship and Love Between Women from the Renaissance to the Present*. New York: William and Morrow Co., 1981.

Nestle, Joan. *A Restricted Country*. Ithaca: Firebrand Books, 1987.

Parkin, Joan and Amanda Posser. "An Academic Affair: The Politics of Butch-Femme Pleasures." *The Persistent Desire: A Femme-Butch Reader*, Joan Nestle, Ed. Boston: Alyson Publications, 1992.

Raymond, Janice. *The Transsexual Empire: The Making of the She-Male*. Boston: Beacon, 1979.

Rich, Adrienne. "Compulsory Heterosexuality and Lesbian Existence (1980)." *Blood, Bread, and Poetry: Selected Prose 1979-1985*. New York: W.W. Norton & Company, 1986.

Sedgwick, Eve. "Epistemology of the Closet." *The Lesbian and Gay Studies Reader*. Henry Abelove, Michelle Aina Barale and David M. Halperin, Eds. New York: Routledge, 1993, pp. 45-61.

Thomson, Rosemarie Garland. *Extraordinary Bodies: Figuring Physical Disability in American Culture and Literature*. New York: Columbia University Press, 1997.

Weeks, Jeffrey. *Sexuality and Its Discontents: Meanings, Myths & Modern Sexualities*. New York: Routledge, 1985.

To(o) Queer or Not?
Queer Theory, Lesbian Community, and the Functions of Sexual Identities

Dana R. Shugar

SUMMARY. While much has been written on the implications of queer theory for lesbian sexuality, little attention has been paid to its impact on lesbian community and subsequent formulations of lesbian identity. The essay argues that theories of identity emerge in part from their interactions with lesbian sexual practice situated within the context of lesbian community. Because lesbian community serves as an important base for socio-political activism, queer theory's destabilization of identity and sexuality has a direct impact on our ability to effect social change. The essay concludes with suggestions for more positive relationships between queer and lesbian communities than have been explored in the past. *[Article copies available for a fee from The Haworth Document Delivery Service: 1-800-342-9678. E-mail address: getinfo@haworthpressinc.com]*

Dana R. Shugar is Associate Professor of English and Women's Studies at the University of Rhode Island. She works in the areas of nineteenth-century British literature, literature by women in the American Left, feminist theory, and the intersections of ethnicity, sexuality, and class identities. Her published works include a book on lesbian separatism along with articles on women's literature, lesbian studies, and nineteenth-century literature. She currently is at work on feminism and the environmental movements as well as a longer study on queer theory.

Address correspondence to: Dana R. Shugar, Women's Studies Program, 90 Lower College Road, Suite 13, University of Rhode Island, Kingston, RI 02881.

[Haworth co-indexing entry note]: "To(o) Queer or Not? Queer Theory, Lesbian Community, and the Functions of Sexual Identities." Shugar, Dana R. Co-published simultaneously in *Journal of Lesbian Studies* (The Haworth Press, Inc.) Vol. 3, No. 3, 1999, pp. 11-20; and: *Lesbian Sex Scandals: Sexual Practices, Identities, and Politics* (ed: Dawn Atkins) The Haworth Press, Inc., 1999, pp. 11-20; and: *Lesbian Sex Scandals: Sexual Practices, Identities, and Politics* (ed: Dawn Atkins) Harrington Park Press, an imprint of The Haworth Press, Inc., 1999, pp. 11-20. Single or multiple copies of this article are available for a fee from The Haworth Document Delivery Service [1-800-342-9678, 9:00 a.m. - 5:00 p.m. (EST). E-mail address: getinfo@haworthpressinc.com].

11

Queer theory has gained quite a lot of attention, use, and critical commentary during the last ten years. Although much has been written on the implications of queer theory for lesbian identity (see, for example, Suzanna Danuta Walters, 1996) and, to a slightly lesser extent, lesbian sexuality (represented by such works as Arlene Stein, 1993 or, in contrast, Sheila Jeffreys, 1994), little attention has been paid to its impact on lesbian community. In this essay, I hope to address a seemingly simple question: What characterizes the relationship between queer theory and lesbian community? The question itself poses several problematic and even false categories, I realize; not the least of which are the terms "queer theory" and "lesbian community." And while attempts to define these terms mean that I necessarily further the dilemma of false categorization, definitions are crucial to our ability to understand the discourse of "queer" and debate its implications for our lives.

Why focus on "lesbian community"? For the purpose of this essay, I define lesbian community as a group or groups of women (I'll leave the definition of "woman" alone for the moment) who are understood, by their sexual and emotional affinities to other women, to be lesbians and who identify, socialize, and organize with similarly defined people in the pursuit of predetermined public or private goals. Many lesbians today debate even the very existence of such a community, much less the difficult, shifting, contentious nature of its borders. Despite the tenuousness of its existence at any historical point, despite its undeniable lack of cohesiveness or unity (indeed, "communi*ties*" is a far more accurate term), and despite doubts about its current efficacy, I contend that lesbian communities have proven valuable to lesbians in a number of ways. While a detailed examination on the formation, continuation, and revisions of lesbian community is beyond the scope of this essay, we do not have to reach far to cite the variety of functions created via lesbian communities: dances, poetry readings, concerts, and the ubiquitous pot-luck spring readily to mind. In the past, communities also have provided familial relations for lesbians alienated from their families of origin, economic opportunities (particularly within separatist collectives), as well as support during times of illness.

Perhaps most relevant to this analysis of queer theory and community, however, is the community's role in socio-political activism. As a group based on socially contentious, sexual identities, lesbian community often serves as a source from which we publicly confront challenges to our sexuality, general well-being, and even our existence. Joshua Gamson details the links between collective identity and community activism:

> Melluci and other theorists of "new social movements" argue more strongly that collective identity is not only necessary for successful collective action, but that it is often an end in itself, as the self-conscious reflexivity of many contemporary movements seem to demonstrate. Collective identity, in this model, is conceptualized as a "continual process of recomposition rather than a given," and "as a dynamic, *emergent* aspect of collective action." (Gamson, 1995:392)

For many members of repressed social groups, "community" becomes one of the most effective means to redress social, political, or economic oppression.

Gamson's comments also direct us to the *interactive* play between the formation of collective identity and community activism. It is here, I argue, that the impact of theory on community is most keenly realized. Although the discourse of "queer" often is positioned as a town-gown split–with academics responsible for the production of theory and those outside college campuses leading the activist vanguard–the production of theories of lesbian identity for at least the last thirty years takes place within activist communities as members simultaneously live out, reassess, and revise the tenets of their theories. Academics themselves often participate in this theory building and activism within these communities as well as within the academy. I hope it is evident that I am not proposing a theory/activism split, here. Rather, it is far more accurate to see the supposed dichotomy as interactive or, better yet, as two faces of the same entity. We do not act outside the realm of theory or ideology, nor does ideology or theory exist outside the realm of experience. As I have discussed elsewhere, for example, women involved in separatist communities of the 1970s and '80s strove to live their lives via the theoretical tenets of radical feminism and lesbian separatism, while they simultaneously authored the on-going production of those discourses (Shugar, 1995:37-107). Given the rather central role that theories of identity enjoy in the production, maintenance, and continuation of lesbian communities, it should come as little surprise that queer theory occupies an important or even contentious location for lesbians today.

While it originated from several different sources, queer discourse made its presence felt particularly during the 1980s through the vehicle of AIDS activism. As Suzanna Walters notes in her essay "From Here to Queer: Radical Feminism, Postmodernism and the Lesbian Menance" (1996), groups such as ACT UP and Queer Nation articulated a radical politics of identity in conjunction with their activism. At the same time, scholars utilized postmodernism and deconstruction, via theorists such as Michel Foucault, to develop queer theory further. The relative youth of queer discourse adds to the difficulties of mapping its borders, though analyses of its theoretical tenets have begun to appear. Judith Butler (1994), for example, explores such germinal works as Gayle Rubin's "Thinking Sex" (1984) and Henry Abelove, David Halperin, and Michele Barale's *The Lesbian and Gay Studies Reader* (1993) in her introduction to the special issue of *differences* on queer theory. Butler contends that queer theory seeks to take sexual practice and sexual difference as its "primary object" even as it relegates the now less-significant factor of gender to feminism (Butler, 1994:1-7). Whatever its positioning of sexuality, queer theory clearly aims to explode the category of sex as society has understood it and strives to see sexual difference as complex nodes of social constructions that are never monolithic, fixed, nor biologically determined. Hence, queer theory often positions identities–sexual and otherwise–as a series of performances in which people choose to engage. As "performativity," sexual identity can be disconnected from other social identities, bodies, or any sort of physical marker. Thus Jacquelyn Zita's exploration of the "male lesbian" (1992) takes place not in the realm of paradox, but in an arena where one identity seems as accessible as any other to any individual.

The re-figuring of sexuality within queer theory also has led to a new understanding of the *historicity* of homosexual identity. Reading primarily from white, western-European experience, theorists such as John D'Emilio (1993) argue that while gay/lesbian sexual practices may have been present, a recognizable homosexual identity did not take shape until the development of capitalism in the nineteenth century. D'Emilio contends that capitalism's transformation of England and United States' demographics from rural to urban centers meant that, for the first time in history, gays and lesbians could forge an identity free from the sexual imperative of procreation and from familial constraint. This freedom, he argues, was necessary for those with homosexual desire to re-fashion that desire into an identity in conjunction with similarly-minded others; acts not possible in the isolated, regimented lives of rural families (D'Emilio, 1993:468-70). With neither sexual practice nor identity existing as fixed objects within queer theory, the perimeters of sexuality (if they remain at all) become far more fluid.

This fluidity of sexuality and identity is both the defining characteristic of queer theory and the crux of its threat to many critics. The theories of lesbian identity that emerged via radical- and lesbian-feminism in the 1960s and 70s directly participated in the construction of lesbian sexual practice, privileging behavior that strove to be egalitarian, non-violent, not overtly promiscuous (though non-monogamy was privileged in some arenas), and that worked against the objectification of women. Works such as Ginny Vida's anthology, *Our Right to Love: A Lesbian Resource Book* (1978), typically structured their topics under such headings as "Lesbian Identity," "Relationships," "Lesbian Activism," and "Sexuality." Interestingly, Vida's anthology includes only three entries under sexuality: an excerpt from Kate Millett's novel *Sita*, an essay on sexual dysfunction, and one "how-to" article that does mention dildo usage and penetration, although it avoids discussion of the more-contested areas of lesbian sexuality. These areas–practices such as butch-femme sexuality (often rejected as "role-playing" or hierarchal relationships), sadomasochism (decried for its incorporation of violence), prostitution, "tricking," or engaging in a multitude of one-night stands (problematized for their emphasis on promiscuity), and the incorporation of pornography into one's sexual play (defined as the objectification of women)–often were marginalized as male-identified or, at the very least, as not feminist. For many lesbians, such practices are simply outside the realm of sexuality as it is constructed through theories of lesbian identity. As the experience of many women in lesbian collectives exemplifies, lesbians took very seriously the task of living out a new, "patriarchy-free" practice of sexuality even as they utilized their experiences of sexuality to further define their theories of identity (Shugar, 1995:61-114). In short, at least for the latter half of the twentieth century, the formulation of theories of lesbian identity has taken place in part as a means both to create and to respond to the experience of lesbian sexual practice.

Queer theory's desire to destabilize identity, then, threatens the constructions of lesbian sexuality as many women have lived them over the past thirty years. Yet, the formulation of queer theory itself is as engaged in the construction of lesbian sexuality, albeit in a radically different form, as was lesbian feminism before it. Indeed, many of queer theory's premises are motivated by the experiences of its proponents within the circle of lesbian feminism. The construction of queer theory is thus an overdetermined act within lesbian communities: queer theory's goals (the destabilization of identity) in part stem from the marginalization of sexual practice crucial in some form to the conceptions of self, or identity, of its practitioners. As a result, the establishment of sadomasochism, butch-femme sexuality, bisexuality, transgendered identities, or simply "queer" sexuality in general within queer theory is not only about the expansion of sexual practice, it is also about the usurpation of lesbian identity as many women have lived it. It should be of little surprise to us, then, that these sites of sexual practice have become hotly contested territory for theorists, as is evinced by the utilization of queer theory in battles over pornography (Judith Butler, 1994), lesbian sadomasochism (Jeffreys, 1994), and butch/femme sexuality (Case, 1997). Depending upon each scholar's position within the discourse, queer theory is cast as either the savior of lesbian sexuality because of its ability to endlessly expand the definitions of what it means to be a sexual lesbian–an approach evident in works such as Lisa Duggan and Nan Hunter's *Sex Wars: Sexual Dissent and Political Culture* (1995)–or, for similar reasons, as the demise of lesbians and lesbianism altogether, as Sheila Jeffreys fears in her essay "The Queer Disappearance of Lesbians" (1994).

While its implications for sexuality are often discussed, the impact that queer theory might have on lesbian community remains relatively unexplored. I contend that the loci of contention with queer theory for sexuality–its desire to expand/explode the boundaries of lesbian identity–are precisely most at issue for lesbian community as well. By opening up what it means to be a lesbian, the erasure of identity as immutable necessarily affects our concepts of lesbian community, in part because we base much of the community's definitions on sexuality and because the practice of sexuality is tied so strongly to the construction of identity theories. Rather than spending much of our energy fighting each other over sexual difference, we can utilize such an opening to include lesbians previously pushed to the margins as a critical part of an alliance against crushing lesbo/homophobia, racism, sexism, or classism.

This opening also creates one of queer theory's largest problems for lesbian community, however, particularly in its practitioners' tendencies to make the category of "lesbian" so ambiguous as to be virtually without meaning in a socio-political context. While such ambiguity undoubtedly proves liberating for many *individuals*, the effect on community, through which women often define their existence and from which activism emerges, is far more troubling. Most problematically, the desire to exist within shifting identities without regard for their cultural values denies the material effects of the power relations at work in society; in other words, identities of race, ethnicity, class, gender, and sexuality are assigned to us whether or not we concur with the designation. And if that identity is less than culturally valuable–if you are of color, not middle- or upper-class, or not male as well as not heterosexual in United States society–your life is materially affected in ways you may not be able to control, despite your wish as a Chicana lesbian, for example, to claim a white-heterosexual male persona.

Scholars such as Rosemary Hennessey (1993) and Sue Ellen Case (1997) have analyzed the impact of queer theory's denial of power hierarchies on women's lives, but what does it mean for lesbian community?

Anti-racist, anti-classist, and anti-sexist work have been important features of lesbian communities during at least the last thirty years, even though the success of that work is often limited. Such commitments shape our activism, as we recognize the need to build alliances and coalitions among ourselves and other oppressed communities and use those bonds to shape our theories further. If we deny the social power that concepts of fixed identities still carry, the goals of our activism are too easily boiled down to, by default, the agendas of white, well-to-do men whose only "difference" resides in sexuality and whose "queer" politics allow them to avoid any analysis of their privilege. Such a movement is evident in the conclusions scholars such as John D'Emilio draw: without an awareness of ethnic/cultural difference, D'Emilio simply misses the current work on gay/lesbian identities (existing in forms different from current constructions) among ancient Native American tribes that certainly pre-dated the nineteenth century (see, for example, Allen, 1986:245-261). This work illuminates different paths to the creations of homosexual identities; paths not dependent upon capitalism, demographic shifts, or the dissolution of extended families. The refusal, born of privilege, to ignore any cultural realities other than those of white, European men at the very least compels us to produce rather incomplete scholarship. It also, through our cultural arrogance, leads us to miss opportunities to form cross-cultural bonds with others who claim homosexual identities and histories.

Such an example demonstrates the conceptual flaws in the scholarly applications of queer theory. But what of our social activism? Groups such as ACT UP and Queer Nation have mobilized highly effective campaigns against HIV and AIDS. Although their messages have had a direct impact through safer-sex campaigns among gay men and successful battles for increased research funding, HIV/AIDS still is one of the fastest growing threats to the lives of *women* of color. We know quite a lot about the transmission and realization of HIV in men's bodies, but we understand far less about the disease vectors or manifestations in women. In the meantime, where are our street demonstrations? Where are our high-profile media events? Where is our commitment?

More pressing for women's health in general is the epidemic of breast cancer in the United States. Estimates of breast cancer risk currently run as high as 1 in every 8 women; some studies show an even higher risk for lesbians as a group (Love, 1995:176-180). As does HIV, this disease crosses race, ethnic, class, and cultural lines and claims far more lesbians' lives than AIDS probably ever will. If queer organizations truly represented the concerns of all their claimed constituency, we should expect to see discussion and activism on diseases such as breast cancer as well as

HIV/AIDS. But where are our street demonstrations? Where are our in-your-face, high-profile media events? Where is our commitment?

Despite my obvious misgivings over its current practice, I do not believe that the problem queer theory presents to lesbian community lies in its analysis of identity as always socially constructed. Indeed, I usually find myself on the front lines of that argument. But queer theory's insistence on identity as a free-floating, interchangeable set of social roles, without regard to the different values society itself places on those roles, leaves us no way *as a community* to conceptualize resistance against larger social forces which continue to devalue women, men of color, working class people, and so on. As Joshua Gamson points out, organized resistance (be it reformist or radical) is often one of the most socially effective functions of oppressed communities (Gamson, 1995:391). Why should we settle for a theoretical construct that conceptually cuts us off from one of our most powerful strategies?

Such questions lead many of us to ask if lesbians, as a community or series of communities, can productively approach queer theory at all. Sheila Jeffreys, for example, takes the position that queer theory, postmodernism, and their lesbian proponents are simply in collusion with gay male interests and, as such, are of little value to lesbian community (Jeffreys, 1994:468-469). This approach, I think, is less than useful: the destabilization of lesbian sexuality and sexual practice within queer theory alone is of value to lesbians if only for the fact that it has provided new ways to think beyond some of the impasses over lesbian identity (particularly played out over sadomasochism, pornography, and butch/femme sexuality) that shredded so many lesbian community projects of the 1970s and '80s. Even the act of destabilization itself enables us to further articulate the borders of our differences, as Evelyn Hammonds points out in her analysis of the implications of queer theory for African-American women's sexuality in "Black (w)holes and the Geometry of Black Female Sexuality" (1994). Queer theory's ability to conceptualize spaces in which transgendered and bisexual women begin to define their lives also remains an important correction to past theories of lesbian identities.

But does our need to incorporate queer theory come at the cost of "community" itself? Perhaps I date myself with such a concern; perhaps the need or desire for a specifically lesbian community is a relic of the past, as the growing popularity of queer organizations among young lesbians in particular might suggest. Yet so much still works against *lesbians* in their various manifestations, specifically because we are marked as both female and homosexual, as well as African, European, Latin, Asian, Native, working class, middle class, along with a variety of other social identities. And the cultural forces that devalue lesbians will not disappear any time soon, even if HIV/AIDS funding finally matches the need, the Defense of Marriage Act (DOMA) is repealed, or the military grants the same rights to its gay/lesbian members as it does to its heterosexual ones. Nor will they disappear even if "queer" becomes thoroughly ensconced in popular culture; indeed, the commodification of queer is fast removing any transformative power it may have had. If queer outrage continues along this path, it—as has rap before it—will become only of use to those who have the most effective marketing strategy. At least as long as lesbians find ourselves besieged in mainstream society, the social, private, and public functions of lesbian communities will remain valuable to many of us.

Despite my misgivings about its efficacy for lesbian community, I do think queer theory shows us one path to broader coalitions and alliances. In this function lies a mutually beneficial relationship: while queer theory offers the hope of a more inclusive community, lesbian and feminist critiques of power differentials provide the much-needed analysis of oppression and privilege sorely lacking within queer theory today. With those understandings, truly effective alliances with gay men's groups, bisexual and transgendered people (identities consigned to no-(wo)man's land within earlier lesbian-feminist constructions), and those who simply consider themselves to be "queer" are within our reach. Given the symbiotic and interactive nature of oppression, alliances and coalitions provide a highly effective way to analyze and strategize against dominant forms of power hierarchies. For this reason alone, lesbian communities might do well to embrace the opportunity queer theory provides of allying with other 'sexual outlaws' (both within and outside the community itself) in a relationship—carefully constructed—that will prove beneficial to all parties. It is important to remember, though, that alliances do not mean the absorption of one group by another; each must come to an understanding of, and respect for, the other's needs and goals before any joint practice can succeed.

However we eventually come to terms with the emergence of queer discourse, the development and practice of theory in general remains an important process in lesbian communities. Despite some of its most vehement detractors within lesbian communities, I do not see queer theory or activism fading from sight in the near future. The popularity that queer theory currently enjoys does not mean that it must or should become lesbian community's "mission statement" in its present form, however. Allying the more positive aspects of both groups—queer theory's radical positioning of sexuality and lesbian/feminism's analyses of hierarchies of power and privilege–can produce one of the most effective strategies against today's oppressive socio-political climate. If we hope to succeed at all, the elimination of that oppression in all its racist, sexist, classist, heterosexist, ableist, and other manifestations, is what we must keep at the forefront of our movements.

REFERENCES

Abelove, Henry, Michele Barale, and David Halperin, eds. *The Lesbian and Gay Studies Reader.* New York: Routledge, 1993.

Allen, Paula Gunn. *The Sacred Hoop: Recovering the Feminine in American Indian Traditions.* Boston: Beacon Press, 1986.

Butler, Judith. "Against Proper Objects." *differences: A Journal of Feminist Cultural Studies* 6.2+3 (1994): 1-26.

Case, Sue Ellen. "Toward a Butch-Feminist Retro-Future." In Heller, Dana, ed. *Cross Purposes: Lesbians, Feminists, and the Limits of Alliances.* Bloomington: Indiana Univ. Press, 1997, 205-220.

D'Emilio, John. "Capitalism and Gay Identity." In *The Lesbian and Gay Studies Reader.* Abelove, Barale, and Halperin, eds., New York: Routledge, 1993, 467-479.

Duggan, Lisa and Nan D. Hunter, eds. *Sex Wars: Sexual Dissent and Political Culture.* New York: Routledge, 1995.

Gamson, Joshua. "Must Identity Movements Self-Destruct? A Queer Dilemma." *Social Problems* 42/3 (August 1995): 390-407.

Hammonds, Evelyn. "Black (w)Holes and the Geometry of Black Female Sexuality." *differences: A Journal of Feminist Cultural Studies* 6.2+3 (1994): 126-145.

Hennessey, Rosemary. "Queer Theory: A Review of the *differences* Special Issue and Wittig's *The Straight Mind.*" *Signs: A Journal of Women and Culture* 18/4 (1993): 964-974.

Jeffreys, Sheila. "The Queer Disappearance of Lesbians: Sexuality in the Academy." *Women's Studies International Forum* 17/5 (1994): 459-472.

Love, Susan. *Dr. Susan Love's Breast Book.* Reading, MA: Addison Wesley, 1995.

Rubin, Gayle. "Thinking Sex: Notes for a Radical Theory of the Politics of Sexuality." In Vance, Carole S., ed., *Pleasure and Danger: Exploring Female Sexuality,* Boston: Routledge and Kegan Paul, 1984, 267-319.

Shugar, Dana R. *Separatism and Women's Community.* Lincoln, NE: University of Nebraska Press, 1995.

Stein, Arlene, ed. *Sisters, Sexperts, Queers: Beyond the Lesbian Nation.* New York: Penguin, 1993.

Vida, Ginny, ed. *Our Right to Love: A Lesbian Resource Book.* New York, NY: Prentice-Hall, 1978.

Walters, Suzanna Danuta. "From Here to Queer: Radical Feminism, Postmodernism, and the Lesbian Menace. (Or, Why Can't a Woman Be More Like a Fag?)" *Signs: A Journal of Women and Culture* 21/4 (Summer 1996): 830-869.

Zita, Jacquelyn N. "The Male Lesbian and the Postmodernist Body." *Hypatia* 7/4 (1992): 106-127.

What Do You Call a Lesbian Who's Only Slept with Men? Answer: Ellen Morgan. Deconstructing the Lesbian Identities of Ellen Morgan and Ellen DeGeneres

Karen Yescavage
Jonathan Alexander

SUMMARY. Lesbian, gay, lesbian-identified bisexual–what do we call women who have sex with other women? What about the character "Ellen," played by actor/comedian Ellen DeGeneres, who identifies as gay but has not (yet?) slept with a woman? Can she legiti-

Karen Yescavage holds a PhD in Psychology and teaches in Psychology and Women's Studies. Her areas of specialty are social psychology, personality, human sexuality, women's studies and ethnic studies. She conducts research on sexual aggression, sexual orientation, and representations of race, gender, and sexuality in U.S. society.

Jonathan Alexander holds a PhD in Comparative Literature and has taught courses in contemporary literature and sexuality. His research interests include Oscar Wilde, queer theory, and nineteenth- and twentieth-century constructions of sexuality. One of his most recent articles is "Out of the Closet and Into the Network: Sexual Orientation and the Computerized Classroom," published in *Computers and Composition*.

Address correspondence to: Karen Yescavage, Department of Psychology, or Jonathan Alexander, Department of English, University of Southern Colorado, 2200 Bonforte Boulevard, Pueblo, CO 81001.

[Haworth co-indexing entry note]: "What Do You Call a Lesbian Who's Only Slept with Men? Answer: Ellen Morgan. Deconstructing the Lesbian Identities of Ellen Morgan and Ellen DeGeneres." Yescavage, Karen, and Jonathan Alexander. Co-published simultaneously in *Journal of Lesbian Studies* (The Haworth Press, Inc.) Vol. 3, No. 3, 1999, pp. 21-31; and: *Lesbian Sex Scandals: Sexual Practices, Identities, and Politics* (ed: Dawn Atkins) The Haworth Press, Inc., 1999, pp. 21-31; and: *Lesbian Sex Scandals: Sexual Practices, Identities, and Politics* (ed: Dawn Atkins) Harrington Park Press, an imprint of The Haworth Press, Inc., 1999, pp. 21-31. Single or multiple copies of this article are available for a fee from The Haworth Document Delivery Service [1-800-342-9678, 9:00 a.m. - 5:00 p.m. (EST). E-mail address: getinfo@haworthpressinc.com].

mately call herself gay? More significantly, what exactly is a "legitimate" lesbian? Further, what does the *Ellen* show tell the millions who viewed the "coming out episodes" about lesbianism? *Ellen* provides an interesting, and highly public, test-case for these questions. This essay will examine three texts: (1) the three "coming-out" episodes, (2) the coverage in the popular press, and (3) the coverage in the queer press. We critique the ways in which the straight and gay communities interpret lesbian identity via their representation of the character "Ellen." *[Article copies available for a fee from The Haworth Document Delivery Service: 1-800-342-9678. E-mail address: getinfo@haworthpressinc.com]*

Like many lesbian, bisexual, and gay people in this country, we watched with excitement and anticipation as Ellen Morgan, the television alter ego of Ellen DeGeneres, came out as lesbian on the hit show, *Ellen*. We knew that DeGeneres, who has had a long and lucrative career as a stand-up comedian and sitcom actor, was taking a huge risk in "outing" both herself–and her character–as gay. But the risk only made the moment more exhilarating. And confusing. For as soon as Ellen Morgan came out, questions popped up. Namely, we were being asked to accept Ellen M. (the television character) as lesbian even though she had never slept with a woman and had only had romantic and sexual relationships with men. What started as a joke (what do you call a lesbian who sleeps with men?) became a series of questions about Ellen M.'s lesbianism.

The lack of clarity about lesbian ontology prompts questions about the use of the word "lesbian," as well as anyone's self-identification as lesbian. For instance, by what right or authority does one say one is lesbian? And why should the self-proclaimed lesbian be believed? For instance, Ellen M. comes out as gay and almost all of the characters believe her automatically; the same is true for Ellen DeGeneres. Why is such self-identification as lesbian almost immediately accepted and largely unquestioned? One wonders what a questioning of such an identity would look like, and why is such questioning seemingly absent in the Ellen M. coming-out episodes and in the Ellen D. press? Further, what does such an absence suggest and reveal about the ways mainstream culture is currently thinking about sexual orientation issues? The primary question is, what do such representations say about us as les-bi-gay people, and about lesbians in particular, and what do we want such representations to say?

In talking about how to answer these questions, we soon discovered that both Ellen the actor and Ellen the character use a very "traditional," binary logic to represent (and "construct") their lesbian identities. First, Ellen M.'s lesbianism is more a function of what she does not want sexually as opposed to what she likes or wishes to affirm in her own life; in other words, she knows she's a lesbian because she doesn't want men. This binary logic (I'm X because I'm not Y) is underscored by two other binary oppositions which the shows deploy to attract attention away from questions of sex: being born gay vs. choosing to be gay and being public about being gay vs. keeping it a private issue. In many ways, the Ellens' coming out reinforces some very traditional understandings of sexual orientation (it's innate and private, for instance), while avoiding more complicated and provocative questions about the role of sexual behavior in human relationships and identity.

Let us start with the role of sex in establishing sexual orientation identity. Most of us come to a "realization" of our same-sex attraction because we experience arousal to a member of the same sex. Or, at least, that's how the standard story goes. One is gay or lesbian because one is *sexually* attracted to one's own sex. With this understanding in mind, then, we would expect to see sexual tension or activity between women as central to a representation of lesbianism. However, when looking at the *Ellen* shows, we were struck by how much sex is *not* a part of the discussion and representation of homosexuality. It is not that Ellen M. is asexual; we know she has been sexual with her old boyfriend, the pizza delivery guy, but we do not know about any past sexual exploration with females.

Her therapy session alludes to some possible crushes she had on girls while she was growing up, but again, no sexual experiences with the same sex are mentioned. While it is completely likely that the writers and producers of the show, as well as DeGeneres herself, may have wanted to "play down" lesbian sexuality for fear of alienating or even disgusting the viewing audience, the show is left with a curious dilemma. How does one represent lesbianism without depicting sexual activity?

In the first three coming-out episodes (aired April 30th, May 7th and May 14th 1997) any opportunity to discuss sex is circumvented and redirected into non-(homo)sexual territory. Ellen M. attempts to use "the sex act" with a man to reaffirm her heterosexuality, which is called into question by her new lesbian friend, Susan. In a further attempt to convince herself that she is indeed straight, Ellen "flaunts" her passion for "man-woman sex" with her friends. Later, however, in a conversation with her therapist, Ellen confesses to having lied to her friends about her romantic tryst. The therapeutic conversation shifts from sex to "clicking"; Ellen undercuts a discussion of sex with a very sentimental plea for someone she can get along with. It sounds as though she were looking for a best friend as opposed to a lover. When the therapist asks her if Ellen has ever clicked with anyone, she responds by saying "Susan," her lesbian friend. Following this lead, Ellen and the therapist discuss the possibility of having a love life with a woman, but again Ellen sidesteps the issue of sexuality by focusing on the social condemnation she might face for living such a "lifestyle."

The remainder of the episode portrays Ellen M. as clicking with Susan. She even goes so far as to proclaim to her friends that she is "in love" with Susan. One might be wondering how love arrives in four days, but what is pertinent is that it has arrived without any sexual expression. Her friends ask her if she has been kissed yet. But Ellen has nothing to report. Indeed, in the remaining two coming-out episodes of the spring season, Ellen concentrates on coming out to family and to her boss, and the question of the place of sexual activity within her new "found" lesbianism is left unanswered.

Ultimately, the absence of sex in these shows prompts us to ask the question, what role does sex with a woman play in determining Ellen M.'s lesbianism? The answer? None. Ellen's "lesbianism" is more a function of what she doesn't want. Thus, we are left wondering at the end of the spring season how Ellen M. defends her claims of lesbianism. Seemingly, the *Ellen* show portrayed for mainstream America that a lack of sexual feeling for men translates into a lesbian identity. She seems comfortable generalizing from one man to all men. Further, without any sexual interactions with Susan, and after only four days of friendship, Ellen *knows* she is lesbian because she can click with this one woman. This leads to a fairly mixed message about the role of sexual behaviors in determining one's sexual identity. On one hand, having sex (or *trying* to have sex) is critical in determining what one is not, i.e., heterosexual, and on the other hand, lack of sex is irrelevant in determining what one is, i.e., lesbian. A crucial question remains: will Ellen be able to generalize this feeling (clicking) to all women just as she generalizes her lack of sexual feelings to all men?

The fall season premiere answers this question within the first five minutes. Ellen M. is on a set-up date with a woman with whom she is clearly not "clicking." Hence, we know that Ellen has not found the immediate cure for her troublesome dating history. Gender is not the only requirement for successful dating; personality will also play a significant, perhaps even determining role. That is to say, not just any woman will turn Ellen on. Big surprise. What the show does play on for surprise, however, is her reunion with her old pizza delivery boyfriend, Dan. With her lesbianism just barely established, Ellen faces a whole new dilemma. Will she fall for Dan the man or will she stay true to her newfound lesbian identity?

In the fall season premiere, she finds herself "clicking," but it's with a guy, a guy with whom she has been sexually intimate. How can this be, she ponders. She even goes so far as to kiss him and slip in several sexual innuendoes of their past sexual history together ("The last time my thighs were that sore was when I was with you").

Ultimately, Ellen M.'s "gayness" is challenged by a kiss with a man–a kiss in which she is clearly an active participant. Can being (hetero)sexual turn her back toward men again? When Dan offers to assist her in the exploration of her feelings, we find the confusion is all cleared up. "Yep, I'm gay," Ellen proclaims with confidence and new-found assurance at the end of the episode. She knows she is gay because of what she does not want. Who better to challenge her lesbianism than a man with whom she "clicks," and with whom she has enjoyed past sexual activity? Still, she has no current desire to sleep with him; therefore, she was right: she is gay!

The confidence of her position, however, is not particularly reassuring. As represented in the show, lesbianism is an identity based on absence, on the absence of sexual desire for men. But this leads to a logical absurdity: how can Ellen M. know whether or not she is lesbian, or asexual, given her criterion for making judgments about her sexual identity? Based on the sexual clicking criterion, it is only fair to ask if Ellen will "know" for sure that she is, in fact, a "real lesbian" when she has sex with a woman. Will prime time television allow Ellen the opportunity to demonstrate her "true" self? What if she tries to have sex with a woman and it doesn't work out? Will she, by definition, be heterosexual again? Based on the sexual orientation model currently represented in the show (lesbianism = absence of desire for men), Ellen M.'s sexual identity is more fluid than she's letting on.

Further, upon more consideration, the lacunae in Ellen M.'s lesbianism open up some serious problems for determining identity based on sexual orientation. For instance, consider the following scene. Ellen tells her gay male friend about her dating frustrations, saying that Dan is the perfect person for her, except he's a guy. Her friend jokingly replies with the possibility of Dan having a sex change. This is a provocative statement. Is Ellen in love with the person? If the "plumbing" were different, would they live happily ever after?

While the shows masterfully skirt issues of sex, they are more than willing to engage less threatening, non-sexual aspects of sexual orientation identity. Specifically, the shows posit that sexual orientation is essentially innate and a fundamentally private (i.e., not political) issue. But the show's grappling with these issues is just as anxiety-ridden as its equivocations about sex, and the episodes ultimately undermine the very positions they are trying to stake out.

Part of the problem arises when Ellen D. decides to write an episode about her character coming out as gay in her mid-thirties. Has Ellen M. been lesbian all along, or does she "decide," much later in life, to become one? The decision DeGeneres ultimately makes reinforces an essentialist position: one is born a lesbian, not made one. Even before the first coming-out episode, DeGeneres speaks about her experience as a lesbian (or as a "gay woman," the term she prefers) in fairly standard clichés. For instance, in the April 30, 1997 interview with Diane Sawyer on *20/20*, DeGeneres comments that being gay is "not contagious" and that "nobody in their right mind would choose something so hard." With such comments, DeGeneres attempts to allay fears of homosexual "recruitment." Simultaneously, *Ellen*, the TV show, uses humor to reinforce the idea that you can't "blame the media" for being gay and that there are no "toaster oven" prizes for recruiting the most women into lesbianism. The message is clear, whether stated seriously, or humorously: homosexuality is not something you can "catch" or be taught; you must be born gay. This stance is augmented by the oft-heard comment that "no one would choose to be gay," which DeGeneres repeats, while emphasizing the use of the word "gay" as opposed to "lesbian" (which to Ellen D., sounds like a "cult" or a "disease").

The essentialist position remains intact throughout the initial coming-out episode. First, Ellen M.'s new friend Susan says that she gets a "gay vibe" from Ellen–the vibe being, perhaps, a signal (picked up by "gaydar") which is only given off by the terminally homosexual. Apparently, one has to be authentically and essentially gay in order to either give off or pick up such vibes. Second, even though Ellen M. is coming to her lesbian identification in her mid-thirties, the show's writers give Ellen a "history" as a woman with past homoerotic feelings. In her discussion with her therapist, Ellen begins to "remember" former crushes, dating all the way back to high school. So, Ellen's "decision" to be gay is not a life-choice as much as it is a coming to terms with feelings which have been there all along.

What is perhaps even more striking is the fact that none of the other characters on the show really question Ellen M.'s identification as lesbian. Even when she makes the "big announcement" to her friends, only Paige, her closest female friend, expresses any amount of incredulity, but her frustration with Ellen revolves primarily around her concern that Ellen has lied to her by not telling her sooner (a fairly cliché position itself). All of her other friends on the show seem to know that Ellen is lesbian even before she does; one of them reports having talked about it to his partner prior to her coming out, and others place bets on what the "big announcement" will be; there is little surprise when someone actually wins the bet. The overall message is clear: Ellen's lesbianism is not a surprise to anyone, except Ellen; only her "outness" is new.

Both Ellens seem insistent that their sexual orientation is not a choice, yet there are curious lapses in the logic with which they both talk about their lesbianism. While the show's essentialist position is fairly dogged, there is one point, in the third episode, where an opening is made to talk about Ellen M.'s "choice." At the end of the show, Ellen and Paige talk about Paige's lack of comfort with Ellen's lesbianism, and Paige, the "good" friend, eventually declares, "I love you whether you're gay, straight, or whatever." Ellen replies comically: "OK–but I'm not sure what whatever is." Paige's follow-up is suggestive: "That's what you were last year." Even though Paige has accepted Ellen as a lesbian, her comment, one of the last heard in the coming-out episodes, suggests that Ellen has not always been lesbian. This small comment problematizes the neatness of the essentialist logic which has dominated the show.

Further contradictions ensue when Ellen D. claims that her lesbianism is a personal affair–a claim she makes on national television. Her comments unwittingly trigger a deconstruction of the "personal" nature of sexual orientation and thus problematize our cultural assumption that sexuality is a purely personal concern. Indeed, the whole question of being "out" begs for a querying of sexual orientation as a private, non-political issue. One of the difficulties with being a lesbian is determining how, where, and when (if ever) to come out to others who most likely have assumed we are heterosexual. However, when we clarify that we are, in fact, not heterosexual, a common, unreflective response is, "Why must you always flaunt your sexuality?" or "Why do you need to come out?" These are not always easy questions to answer, especially when under attack. That Ellen DeGeneres addresses this latter question in front of the nation's critical gaze is courageous. However, it's also confusing.

Specifically, Ellen D.'s reasons for coming out problematize her separation of the private and public, the personal and political. Originally, in the *Time* article, Ellen says,

> I always thought I could keep my personal life separated from my professional life. In every interview I ever did, everyone tried to trap me into saying I was gay. I learned every way to dodge that or if they just blatantly asked me, I would say I don't talk about my personal life. I mean, I really tried to figure out every way to avoid answering that question for as long as I could. (Handy, 1997:80)

The article goes on to say that this became a lot harder in September, after news leaked out that she wanted to have the character she played on television discover she is a lesbian. These types of comments are indicative of her assumption that there is a clear distinction between one's personal and public selves. According to her comments, Ellen D. assumes her sexual orientation to be merely a personal identity, and unfortunately, one she simply can no longer keep private. She of course is not alone in this assumption. For instance, in a letter to the editor the following week in *Time*, one reader states, "It's none of my business if DeGeneres is gay, and I don't like her trying to make it my business. DeGeneres, keep your private life private or get help" (*Time*, 1997:9). Additionally, on *Oprah*, one of the audience members challenges the cover story of *Time*, saying, "Why do you need to come out to everyone saying 'yep, I'm gay?' You don't see me saying to everyone 'yep, I'm straight.'" However, in her television interview on *20/20*, there is a subtle slippage in her dialogue about coming out. She remarks to Diane Sawyer, "I made the decision in the summer that I wasn't going to live my life as a lie anymore." This is juxtaposed rather poignantly with a short clip from one of her stand-up comedy routines where she talks about going out with a lot of men—a reminder to the viewing audience of her former life in the closet.

Ellen D., we might surmise, would prefer to keep her lesbianism a "private" issue, and yet, she no longer wants to "live a lie." The contradiction comes into focus when Ellen realizes that the private and public selves are not mutually exclusive. In other words, if her lesbian identity were purely private, then she would not feel as though she had been living her life as a lie.

The public/private tension becomes even more fascinating when politics come into play. In talking with Diane Sawyer, Ellen D. comments, "The main reason I never wanted to do this [i.e., come out] is because I don't want to become political and I don't want to become some gay activist." She continues by saying, "It's just about my personal story." Then, in a rather schizoid instant, Ellen parallels her life with that of Rosa Parks, detailing how Rosa was "an ordinary person who wouldn't be belittled for what she couldn't change." Ellen, who just moments earlier says she doesn't want to become political, declares "I wasn't going to sit on the back of the bus anymore. I belong with everybody else. And that's what I finally did." Ellen wants to assimilate, but she can't because her "private" life, she is finding, is not so privately constructed. Her analogies betray her: she would like to blend in on the bus and say out loud, "Yep, I'm gay."

While much of the mainstream media coverage reflects Ellen D.'s de-

sire to mute the politics of her coming out, most of the queer press expresses frustration at her assimilationist stance. For instance, the cover story
pictures and titles chosen for each of the three magazines that portrayed
Ellen around the time of her coming out are telling. First, there is the now-
famous *Time* cover where Ellen says boldly, "Yep, I'm gay." At first
glance, one might see a confident woman making the declaration of the
decade. A more critical gaze detects her dubious posture and angle of the
lens. Ellen is (1) squatting down, (2) looking up slightly into the viewers'
eyes, and (3) wearing a big smile on her face. These three things taken
together seem to be saying to the nation through one of the leading mainstream magazines: I'm not pushing any agenda, I'm submissive, and
please like me, I'm still "the girl-next-door."

When we turn our attention to one of the most popular queer magazines, *Out*, we get a very different impression of Ellen D.'s lesbian identity. Simply put, Ellen is being mocked. The title reads, "Come on out,
Ellen, the water's just fine!" The cover of the magazine satirizes her by
presenting a caricature with a very tentative-looking face, whose toe is just
barely touching the water and whose hand is definitely posed, saying
"don't rush me." This is quite a telling choice given that the cover story
and picture were printed a month after Ellen had posed for the cover of
Time.

Even more telling is the lack of cover story altogether by *The Advocate*,
"The National Gay and Lesbian Magazine." In June, however, there is a
cover story that says "Lesbian celebrities are leading the way out of the
show business closet . . . so where are the men?" (Gallagher 1997:26).
While men's absence from the public eye is being scrutinized, a sexist
metaphor equating strength and courage with male genitalia is offered to
"praise" Ellen for the guts it took for her to come out: "not many enter-
tainers with that kind of influence and visibility have had the balls to say
publicly,'I'm gay.'" Feint praise indeed.

Finally, the cover of a new magazine specifically for lesbians was the
least harsh on Ellen D. The cover of *Girlfriends*, "America's fastest-grow-
ing lesbian magazine," has a photo of Ellen on the set of her show where
she is surrounded by her staff who are busy helping her get her hair and
make-up ready for her big coming-out episode. The cover reads "Coming
Out Under Fire," a peculiar choice given the picture they chose to accompany it. Ellen is barely recognizable in the photo; she is clearly distraught,
which matches the article's title, but the picture depicts her less like a
soldier in a war zone than a misfit in a fashion show. The picture is just as
much, if not more, about her staff trying to make her look good, rather than
being about any major political statement she is about to make. One gets

the impression that *Girlfriends* is about just that–mindless girlfriends who play with each other's hair and make-up, rather than with political ideas.

At this point, one might be tempted to ask why Ellen DeGeneres has gone to such great lengths to represent herself and her character as innately and "privately" gay–especially since there is enough slippage in the representation to warrant some serious questioning, and "queerying," of her lesbian "performance." The answer is simple: her representation is the least threatening to a potentially very resistant audience. It is also understandable given our society's heteronormativity–and fear of explicit same-sex sexuality. Ellen's lesbianism makes more sense if she can't help herself; after all, how else can a heteronormative culture explain why someone would not act, talk, and represent oneself as anything but "straight," i.e., normal?

But it is also understandable at a more personal level. Ellen D.'s plea for acceptance is one which most of us can identify with: this is how I am; please don't hate me for being myself. And, in a world in which, as Foucault has pointed out, sexuality is identity, it is necessary for one's sexual orientation to be "stable" in order for one's identity, one's sense of self, to be stable (Foucault, 1978:35). When that stability is problematized (by bisexuality, by the gap between experience and label, by the political consequences of that which we want to be personal and non-political), then we are faced with the more difficult and anxiety-provoking task of having to choose, and continually construct, our identities. In terms of the subject at hand, both Ellen M. and Ellen D. want to (re)present themselves as "biologically" given, but, upon closer examination, it is evident that conscious decisions and political commitments are being made.

Indeed, our analysis of the *Ellen* shows reveals the shifts, subtle as they are, being made in the popular understanding of lesbianism and sexual orientation–shifts which indicate the cracks and fault lines in essentialist thinking about sexuality and identity. What is most exciting to us about these fault lines is that they are occurring in a popular medium, a series of television shows, which are our culture's primary reflection–and construction–of how we think of ourselves.

REFERENCES

20/20. CBS, KKTV, Channel 11, Pueblo, CO. 30 April 1997.

Cover Illustration. "Yep, I'm Gay." *Time*, 14 April 1997.

Cover Illustration. "Come on Out, Ellen! The Water's Just Fine!" *Out*, May 1997: 68-69, 126-127.

Cover Illustration. "Coming Out Under Fire: On the Set of Ellen," *Girlfriends*, May/June 1997: 36-37.

Ellen. CBS, KKTV, Channel 11, Pueblo, CO. 30 April 1997.

Ellen. CBS, KKTV, Channel 11, Pueblo, CO. 7 May 1997.

Ellen. CBS, KKTV, Channel 11, Pueblo, CO. 14 May 1997.

Foucault, Michel. *The History of Sexuality: An Introduction.* Volume 1. Trans. by Robert Hurley. New York: Vintage, 1978.

Gallagher, John. "The Amazing Invisible Men of Show Business," *The Advocate* 13 May 1997: 26-33.

Handy, Bruce. "Yep, I'm Gay," *Time,* 14 April 1997: 78-86.

"Letters to the Editor." *Time,* 5 May 1997: 8.

Oprah. CBS, KKTV, Channel 11, Pueblo, CO. 30 April 1997.

Oprah. CBS, KKTV, Channel 11, Pueblo, CO. 7 May 1997.

To Love Women, or To Not Love Men: Chronicles of Lesbian Identification

Hinda Seif

SUMMARY. A discussion of the ways three women of the San Francisco Bay Area navigate their attractions and identifications, and the reasoning behind and consequences of their choices. Donna is attracted to women and men and identifies as lesbian; Dahlia identifies as a bisexual lesbian; Aviva used to identify as lesbian and now calls herself as a lesbian-identified bisexual woman. Their ideologies are compared, and the interaction of their race, ethnicity, and sexual identification is also discussed. *[Article copies available for a fee from The Haworth Document Delivery Service: 1-800-342-9678. E-mail address: getinfo@haworthpressinc.com]*

Over the past decade, there has been increasing discussion about the social construction of sexual identification labels (Garber, 1995; Rust, 1993; Phelan, 1994). This debate has eroded essentialist assumptions that we are born only attracted to men or women, and called into question the

---

Hinda Seif, MA Women's Studies, is a doctoral student of Anthropology at U. C. Davis and advisory board member of *Bridges: A Journal for Jewish Feminists and Our Friends*.

Address correspondence to: Hinda Seif, Department of Anthropology, University of California Davis, Davis, CA 95616-8522.

The author gives special thanks to the Charles and Gertrude Gordon Foundation, the University of Arizona Department of Women's Studies, Susan Philips, Myra Dinnerstein, and Janet Jakobsen.

[Haworth co-indexing entry note]: "To Love Women, or To Not Love Men: Chronicles of Lesbian Identification." Seif, Hinda. Co-published simultaneously in *Journal of Lesbian Studies* (The Haworth Press, Inc.) Vol. 3, No. 3, 1999, pp. 33-44; and: *Lesbian Sex Scandals: Sexual Practices, Identities, and Politics* (ed: Dawn Atkins) The Haworth Press, Inc., 1999, pp. 33-44; and: *Lesbian Sex Scandals: Sexual Practices, Identities, and Politics* (ed: Dawn Atkins) Harrington Park Press, an imprint of The Haworth Press, Inc., 1999, pp. 33-44. Single or multiple copies of this article are available for a fee from The Haworth Document Delivery Service [1-800-342-9678, 9:00 a.m. - 5:00 p.m. (EST). E-mail address: getinfo@haworthpressinc.com].

twin psychological paradigms of heterosexual and homosexual identity development which create linear congruence from often multiple attractions. These early identity models neatly conclude with the discovery of one's sexual essence through introspection, where one is attracted to either the same or the opposite sex and lives happily ever after (Rust, 1993: 51-53).

Yet our desires and sexual expressions are often not as straightforward; in the words of sexual theorist Marjorie Garber, "Eroticism is what escapes, what transgresses rules, breaks down categories, questions boundaries. It cannot be captured in a manual, a chart, a lab test, a manifesto" (1995:160). In her study of attitudes about bisexual women in the lesbian community, sociologist Paula Rust points out that the identity histories of lesbians in the United States include more variation than one might expect. One of three of the participants in her study has wondered if she were bisexual since identifying as a lesbian (1995:59).[1] These chronicles of identity offer a hint of the diverse desires and sexual involvements of women who call themselves lesbians.

I recount the experiences and feelings of three people who currently call themselves lesbian or lesbian-identified in order to explore the ways that these women manage their desires toward other-sexed people. These college-educated interviewees identify as a lesbian, a bisexual lesbian, and a lesbian-identified bisexual woman.

In this brief exploration, I do not pretend to address the myriad cultural variations on lesbian identification. One participant comes from working class and two from middle class backgrounds; two identify as European-American Ashkenazi Jews, a third as a woman of African American and Ashkenazi heritage. Queer theorist Elias Farajeje-Jones reminds us of the ways that the term "lesbian" may have different meanings depending on one's cultural situation (1995:122). The term "lesbian" is of European origin, yet woman-to-woman desire and love has origins, expressions, and terminologies that are grounded in various geographies and cultures.

While this piece focuses upon the love of lesbians for people across genders, I do not wish to give the impression that all lesbians desire men or overemphasize the importance of cross-gender desire within lesbian communities. Clearly, the center of lesbianism is love for women. Yet, as other desires lie at the periphery of lesbian lives and energies, an inability to integrate these feelings and a tendency to "police" them may become divisive and damaging to lesbian vitality and sexual expression (Armstrong, 1995:216). Rather than perpetuate lesbian/bisexual antagonism, it is important to acknowledge the mentoring, friendship, and love that I and many bisexual women have received from the many lesbians in our lives.

In usual academic fashion, I searched for common threads linking the perspectives of each interviewee. Different participants discuss the suppression of overt desire toward men in some lesbian communities and their own internalized "biphobia," the importance in their lives of social acceptance within lesbian community, and the nourishment that they have gained from this alliance. They betray a problematic tendency to see bisexuality in more "natural" terms and lesbianism as more of a social/political alignment, as they simultaneously question current paradigms of sex, gender, and sexual orientation. They also relate their specific choice to place women first in their lives on a political, emotional, and sexual level. Yet I am struck and delighted by the great variation between their histories, the ways that each identifies sexually, and the decisions that they make and philosophies that each has developed to creatively and ethically support their sexual desires, practices, and namings.

Since the three women range in age from late 30s to mid-40s, they depict their lesbian origins in the '70s and early '80s and their peer groups. One of the participants, Aviva, remarks on recent changes that she sees among Bay Area lesbians, including a greater tolerance of and openness toward the expression of different desires among lesbians and others.

DONNA

Donna is a high school teacher in her early forties. "My sexual preference lies somewhere in the middle of that Kinsey scale in that I am attracted to men and women with a leaning towards women." She was married for years to a man prior to having sexual relationships with women since the age of 30. Donna considers herself a "bisexual who identifies as a lesbian," a "little b bisexual" who does not call herself bisexual publicly, as differentiated from what she considers "big B bisexual[s, who] . . . go to bisexual groups . . . [and] . . . have friends that identify as bisexual."

Donna makes a conscious decision to use the identifying term "lesbian" in order to claim membership in her community of choice, lesbian community. "I socialize with lesbians mostly–I go to lesbian events, and I am in a lesbian relationship. If I was single, I would probably still move in lesbian circles and look to find a female lover." She presents bisexuality as more of her essence, and lesbianism as a social term that she uses to express community affiliation.

Donna recounts events and offers a number of reasons that have reinforced her decision to identify as lesbian and mostly keep quiet about her attractions to men. One episode which stands out occurred during an early date with a woman who became a long-term partner:

> When I was first going out with my last lover, I mentioned to her that I was bisexual. And she said that she was going to break up with me if I said that again. . . . She had been in the lesbian community for many years and identified as a very strong lesbian, and really had all that bisexual phobia, and really didn't want to associate with any-body who was bisexual. Even with friends. And so I . . . thought it was best to just drop the whole bisexual piece.

It is noteworthy that Donna's girlfriend did not question the fact of Donna's attractions; she would tolerate them if Donna did not discuss them and called herself a lesbian. The commonality of lesbian attraction and sexual history with men, which was accepted if talked about in "hushed tones" but jeopardized one's friendships and community standing if one were "outspoken about it," was a recurring theme in Donna's conversation.

Donna explains that she has seen much "biphobia" in the lesbian communities around her, and that declaring oneself bisexual or discussing one's attractions to men may jeopardize one's opportunities to date les-bians. She believes this stigma is partly related to an association between bisexuality and HIV transmission. Donna realizes that this emotional con-nection is spurious, and that fears of bisexuals are often irrational and illogical.

> A lot of lesbian women don't want to date bisexual women. . . . Somehow it's very taboo in the lesbian community. . . . [P]eople who I know . . . both in the straight community and in the gay community very often will mix who they have sex with but still identify as either straight or gay or lesbian. . . . And people associate . . . bisexuality with AIDS. . . . Which really . . . is just as true for all people who practice unsafe sex. . . . I know that logically . . . anyway.

Donna admits that she is also reluctant to date bisexual women and prefers to date lesbians:

> [W]hen I think of bisexuals—and this is a terrible . . . I kind of think of them as not being able to make up their minds. . . . On an emotion-al level there's a whole bunch of stigma associated with bisexuality. . . . And . . . I haven't resolved that. I know that that's my stuff, I know that that's not really based in logic. . . . It may be also coming to terms with who I am.

As Donna recounts the reluctance of many lesbians, including herself, to date and socialize with women who call themselves bisexual, she also shares that some lesbians are supportive of her expression of her desires. According to Donna, this acceptance may be related to different cultural expressions of lesbianism and homoeroticism including traditional butch/fem roles:

> I had been with another woman who . . . was older . . . and who was very accepting of me being bisexual. [I]n fact [she] said that she only dated bisexual women. . . . She was a Latina and very butch, and she liked very fem women. . . . My lover right now doesn't mind if I call myself bisexual. . . . I have this fascination for Gregory Hines . . . I think he's really hot. And I've talked about him . . . and . . . she doesn't seem to mind. I think that she accepts that part of me and understands that I'm monogamous and I'm not going to be running off with someone else. I mean, I'm certainly not going to be running off with Gregory Hines.

Donna's honest exploration of her desires has been hampered in her search for counseling services as well as in her social circles:

> When I was breaking up with my last lover . . . I . . . interviewed with a therapist who had ongoing therapy groups. And she . . . separated them into mixed [women and] lesbian. . . . I . . . wanted to join a lesbian group, but I shared with her in the initial interview that I was open to dating men. 'Cause I was just breaking up with my lover and I was thinking . . . , well, if a nice guy came along . . . I just might consider it, you know? And that was something I was also coming to terms with. . . . So I said it would be good if I could talk about it. But she said that I can come into the mixed group because then I wasn't really lesbian. . . . I became very upset.

The therapist's assessment did not preclude Donna from joining the lesbian therapy group. Reminiscent of the deal she struck with her former girlfriend, Donna could attend that group as long as she would not talk about her attractions to men there. Her feelings for men are an unresolved "problem" that Donna is unable to discuss in therapy:

> I went into [the] lesbian therapy group and I haven't talked about any of my bisexual feelings while there. . . . Obviously it's a problem that I haven't integrated. Because I can't talk about it in therapy, which is crazy, but I really feel very uncomfortable since I was told . . . from

the beginning that if I talk about my attractions to men in the therapy group people will not be supportive. Okay. . . . Maybe it's not an issue for [the other group members]. I don't know.

Donna also sees much self-censorship in her lesbian[s] community:

I know plenty of women who are attracted to men and who are lesbians and who get very nervous when that happens. I had one friend in particular who would call me, very anxious about having hugged this man who she became attracted to and spent a lot of time with. . . .

Donna's sense of isolation and lack of opportunity to express the spectrum of her sexual feelings were epitomized by her concluding remarks to the interviewer: "And this has also been helpful, to talk to you, because it gives me a place to talk about it."

DAHLIA

Dahlia is a health care worker in her early forties who identifies as a bisexual lesbian and a single parent. She explains that she is "naturally" attracted to both women and men, depicting her bisexuality as an organic identification. Her lesbianism is more politically motivated and represents a conscious choice about the direction in which she wishes to steer her sexuality and relationships.

I feel that if people are born anything, I was born bisexual. . . . I have fallen in love with people of both genders. . . . My fantasies go towards both genders. . . . And so I have the capacity to love, both emotionally, physically, . . . a person, because of their individual qualities regardless of what gender they are. So that's the bisexual part.

Dahlia has numerous reasons for calling herself a "bisexual lesbian" rather than a bisexual woman. Similar to Donna, a lesbian community is Dahlia's social community of choice; she is part of a community of lesbians of color. Her lesbian identification is a way to maintain membership in this community; sexual involvement or partnership with a man would jeopardize her standing in this community:

Why I add the "lesbian" is really more the question than why I add the "bisexual." . . . I guess part of it may be a refusal to let go of the lesbian community and my place in it.

Dahlia seeks membership in the lesbian community because she feels the smaller bisexual community offers too few resources and possibilities for interaction with other people of color:

> The bisexual community [is] . . . still not at a size where I feel that it can give me the level of support that the lesbian community can. It just doesn't have the resources at this point in time. . . . But as it's been growing, it's come to look more and more feasible as a community that I could call home and feel that it was giving me what I needed. . . .

As a woman of mixed heritage who was raised by an activist mother, Dahlia also believes that it is important for her to primarily identify with the aspects of her identity that are most embattled in the 1990s United States. After being primarily raised by her Jewish mother in a single parent household, Dahlia spent her young adulthood immersing herself in African American culture. Likewise, Dahlia publicly emphasizes her lesbian side, or her attractions to women, over her attractions to men:

> Being raised politically . . . I felt it more important to identify with the portions . . . of myself that were the more oppressed group. . . . Even though all these concepts are all really incredible nonsense, and ultimately we're all just human beings that are made up of many genes which don't really have any racial designations. . . . Both the ethnic labels . . . have no real basis in scientific fact, and the sexual orientation [labels] are for the most part a human creation as well. Perhaps some people are born totally heterosexual and perhaps some people are born totally homosexual, but I would say the vast majority of us have put . . . labels and categories and restrictions on ourselves based on society's conditioning and on decisions and how to deal with the society we live in and how to deal with our own desires. . . . The majority of us are not only bisexual or pansexual, but . . . the majority of us change over time. . . . But given the political and social realities, we have to deal with all this nonsense. So as far as where I am in the whole ethnic construct . . . and the communities that I was born a part of . . . it felt more important to identify with the African American part than with the Jewish part. . . . Similarly in terms of claiming lesbian and gay identity.

Dahlia also chooses to identify as lesbian because she feels that she has a better chance of building a healthy, egalitarian relationship with a woman. Using this term defines who she is looking for in a partnership, and perhaps makes it more likely that she will find a woman partner:

Why I add the "lesbian" is . . . also I . . . made a decision . . . that I really would rather be with a woman. And the reasons [I would rather be with a woman] are *not just* so the lesbian community won't reject me, but also because I felt that my chances of having the kind of relationship I want are much *greater* with a woman. That women . . . tend to be more advanced in terms of relationship . . . and therefore pull more of their weight. . . . There's still . . . somewhere between one and ten percent space left open in case I meet this . . . as-close-to-perfect-as-any-human-being-could-be-person . . . and it just happens to be a man. . . . So that's why I say I'm a bisexual lesbian, it's because I made this *decision* to actively look for a female partner and try not to fall in love with a man.

Echoing the sentiments of Donna, Dahlia shares that while she is anxious for the lesbian community to accept what she considers the "bisexual" aspects of her identity and sexual feelings, she realizes that she is reluctant to date women who identify as bisexual:

I have some internalized biphobia . . . from decades of working for the lesbian and gay community. . . . I eventually confronted the fact that even though I wanted people to accept me completely as bisexual . . . , at the same time I had that same fear that other lesbians have of dating a bisexual woman. I thought she'd leave me for a man, and I couldn't believe that I would have that attitude–that she wasn't really serious about being in a relationship with a woman. So I wanted to be accepted as a bisexual but I wanted a relationship with a lesbian.

Dahlia proudly claims a lesbian identification and sees no incompatibility between her understanding of this term and her attractions to men. She eloquently explains that lesbianism is an affirmative expression of her love for women:

[T]he other reason I claim my lesbianism is because something in me continues to insist on defining lesbianism as women who love women rather than as women who reject men. I think that loving women should be the primary definition of lesbianism, that . . . [it] should be based on a positive, not a negative. . . . I think if more lesbians can see that argument, I'm sure most . . . , even lesbians who have no interest in men whatsoever, would prefer to be defined as lesbians because they love women, not because they don't love men.

AVIVA

Aviva is a Jewish community worker in her mid-30s who considers herself a lesbian-identified bisexual. She is in a non-monogamous relationship and her primary partner is a woman. Aviva has shifted her sexual identification three times since her college years:

> In terms of my history, I came out at twenty as bisexual. . . . That felt easy, like of course I've always been attracted to both women and men. . . .

Soon after, Aviva changed her identification to that of "lesbian." Like the first two interviewees, this identification was partly a strategic move meant to establish her place in a loving, supportive lesbian community. Yet she was also concerned about the "rigidity" of lesbian culture at her college in the late '70s. While Aviva's earlier process of coming out as bisexual is presented as "easy," her subsequent switch to a lesbian identification is described in conflicted terms:

> [At] that time, there was a lot of pressure to be either lesbian or straight, there wasn't a lot of room to be bisexual. . . . The community I was in at college was very small, was very tight, and I needed that support, I needed that community, I needed the love. . . . So I was very susceptible to that pressure, and I came out as lesbian a year later. . . . Mostly the biggest struggle for me about coming out as lesbian is that . . . that community . . . looked stifling, it looked rigid, it looked like I would have to conform. . . . You would have to dress a certain way and talk a certain way. . . . There wasn't as much room back then in terms of what a lesbian could be or look like. . . .

Aviva traded a certain degree of conformity to the norms of her lesbian community for love and acceptance. Yet she also describes the great personal development that she experienced from claiming a strong lesbian identification. With the help of her friends and lesbian ideology, she was able to counteract some of her androcentric upbringing and firmly put women first in her life:

> [A]t the same time I could see the potential for a lot of growth. . . . Feeling like I could define myself sexually the way I wanted. I didn't have to play games, I didn't have to go passive with men, I didn't have to be nice to men. There just was this liberation. . . . It was an important stage for me. Because men had come first for me, I . . .

looked to men as role models . . . I had to undo that conditioning and coming out as a lesbian was really important.

In contradiction to theories of lesbian identity development which see coming out as a lesbian as the end point, Aviva describes her decade of lesbian identification as a "stage." She currently calls herself a lesbian-identified bisexual.[1] She described the way this most recent turn in identification was instigated by her feelings of solidarity with a bisexual woman friend who was in a relationship with a man rather than by any change in her own sexual desires or practices. When friction erupted in her Jewish women's prayer group, Aviva sided with her friend:

> I was part of . . . a small Jewish lesbian and bisexual women's Havurah, but it was basically all lesbians except for one, who was having a big struggle about it with the group. I was witnessing that and . . . that was part of my . . . unconsciously moving in that direction. Trying to be an ally to this friend. . . . And that was painful for me and made me really upset and angry. . . . So that [group] fell apart . . . over biphobia. . . .

After the disturbing disintegration of her family of choice, Aviva's newer friends were less likely to identify as lesbians. "My community became more queer rather than more lesbian. Which has its pros and cons. . . . " She currently socializes with more men and more people in cross-gender relationships than she did previously.

When Aviva fell in love and became sexually involved with a man, she reclaimed a bisexual identity. Unlike Donna and Dahlia, who present their bisexuality as more natural than their lesbianism, Aviva explains that her current identification is a strategic choice which she may change in the future. At this stage in her life sexual liberation is key, and she feels that bisexual affiliation currently offers more opportunities to her. The form of sexual liberation that Aviva seeks has also changed over time:

> Bisexuality–it means more freedom. When I came out as a lesbian, it was the liberatory step for me. And then. . . . coming out as bisexual was a liberatory step. . . . I feel like it allowed me to define my sexuality in the way that I wanted to define it. . . . I can choose to be sexual with whomever, whenever, however. There's a lot of room in bisexual communities. *There's more emphasis on sexual liberation in and of itself, and that's been exciting for me.* . . . Now it's still a box. . . . [T]here's a way that we're still at a point in time where we need boxes, as much as we all might like to say we don't. And this

one feels bigger than the others for me right now. It's . . . strategic, just like being a lesbian was. I don't feel like it's anything so sacred or innate. . . . It's very conditioned by who I am and the times . . . , and for me it's about . . . allowing me the most freedom at this time. And it could change. . . .

Aviva states that she "can choose to love men . . . and know deep down that women are going to come first." Yet she also notes the losses that resulted from her distancing from lesbian communities, and the inclusion of more men in her social circles:

Me and [my primarily partner] have been talking about this lately, we've been missing lesbians in our lives, or lesbian-identified bi-sexuals. Because [we] are both that way, we both pretty much put women first and are with women sexually. And most of our inner circle . . . is bisexual but in cross-gender relationships, and more inclined that way. . . . I have personally . . . gained a lot from connecting with men. I love being in mixed gender community, and I want that in my life. I think we do have to watch for the sexism because it ain't disappeared. . . .

These narratives remind us that lesbianism is an affirmative love for and valuation of women, a movement that is opposed to "the attitudes of homophobia, racism and sexism" rather than one that "define[s its] enemy as 'straight, white men'" (Highleyman 1995:75). This vision allows for a fuller acknowledgment of the sexual histories and desires of those who claim the identity that will ultimately move, in the words of lesbian political theorist Shane Phelan, "from the logic of exclusion through demarcation to a logic of inclusion, enlarging both the community and meaning of lesbianism" (1994:97).

NOTE

1. Aviva's decision to call herself a lesbian-identified bisexual differs from that of another interviewee, Leah. A strong feminist who is non-monogamous and is primarily partnered with a lesbian, Leah explains why she decided to rename herself from "lesbian-identified bisexual" to "just bisexual" a few years ago:

I know that I can call myself bisexual with confidence and not question my own commitment to women. It used to be that I had to say the word lesbian I think to prove to other people and myself how committed I was. . . .

REFERENCES

Armstrong, Elizabeth. "Traitors to the Cause? Understanding the Lesbian/Gay 'Bisexuality Debates.'" *Bisexual Politics: Theories, Queries, and Visions*. Ed. Naomi Tucker. New York: Harrington Park Press, 1995. 199-217.

Farajeje-Jones, Elias. "Fluid Desire: Race, HIV/AIDS, and Bisexual Politics." *Bisexual Politics: Theories, Queries, and Visions*. Ed. Naomi Tucker. New York: Harrington Park Press, 1995. 119-130.

Garber, Marjorie. *Vice Versa: Bisexuality and the Eroticism of Everyday Life*. New York: Simon and Schuster, 1995.

Highleyman, Liz A. "Identity and Ideas: Strategies for Bisexuals." *Bisexual Politics: Theories, Queries, and Visions*. Ed. Naomi Tucker. New York: Harrington Park Press, 1995. 73-92.

Phelan, Shane. *Getting Specific: Postmodern Lesbian Politics*. Minneapolis: University of Minnesota Press, 1994.

Rust, Paula C. *Bisexuality and the Challenge to Lesbian Politics: Sex, Loyalty, and Revolution*. New York: New York University Press, 1995.

_____ . "'Coming Out' in the Age of Social Constructionism: Sexual Identity Formation among Lesbian and Bisexual Women." *Gender & Society* 7.1 (March 1993): 50- 79.

'Without Contraries Is No Progression': S/M, Bi-nary Thinking, and the Lesbian Purity Test

Atara Stein

SUMMARY. Some lesbians subject other queer women to a type of purity test, stereotyping bisexuals, transsexuals, and leatherwomen as threats to the lesbian and feminist movements. Such attitudes frequently reveal rigid, binary, either-or thinking and an intolerance of difference. This essay, by contrast, argues in favor of an embrace of diversity within the queer women's community and examines the way bisexuals, transsexuals, and leatherwomen exhibit a resistance to binary thinking and a "tolerance for ambiguity." *[Article copies available for a fee from The Haworth Document Delivery Service: 1-800-342-9678. E-mail address: getinfo@haworthpressinc.com]*

I always thought the world was divided into only two kinds of people–those who think the world is divided into only two kinds of people, and those who don't.

–Molly Ivins

Atara Stein is Associate Professor of English Literature at California State University Fullerton. She received her PhD from UCLA. She is currently working on a book called *Romanticism and Popular Culture.*

Address correspondence to: Atara Stein, Department of English, California State University–Fullerton, Fullerton, CA 92834.

[Haworth co-indexing entry note]: "'Without Contraries Is No Progression': S/M, Bi-nary Thinking, and the Lesbian Purity Test." Stein, Atara. Co-published simultaneously in *Journal of Lesbian Studies* (The Haworth Press, Inc.) Vol. 3, No. 3, 1999, pp. 45-59; and: *Lesbian Sex Scandals: Sexual Practices, Identities, and Politics* (ed: Dawn Atkins) The Haworth Press, Inc., 1999, pp. 45-59; and: *Lesbian Sex Scandals: Sexual Practices, Identities, and Politics* (ed: Dawn Atkins) Harrington Park Press, an imprint of The Haworth Press, Inc., 1999, pp. 45-59. Single or multiple copies of this article are available for a fee from The Haworth Document Delivery Service [1-800-342-9678, 9:00 a.m. - 5:00 p.m. (EST). E-mail address: getinfo@haworthpressinc.com].

45

In *The Lesbian Body*, Monique Wittig postulates transcending "stupid duality," exhorting, "may your understanding embrace the complexity of the play of the stars and of the feminine agglomerations, may you yourself in this place strive in a frenzied confrontation whether in the shape of the angel or the shape of the demon" (1986:145). Similarly, in "La conciencia de la mestiza: Towards a New Consciousness," Gloria Anzaldúa calls for "a tolerance for contradictions, a tolerance for ambiguity," which has "produced both a creature of darkness and a creature of light, but also a creature that questions the definitions of light and dark and gives them new meanings" (1987:79-81). And in "Imitation and Gender Insubordination," Judith Butler states, "I'm permanently troubled by identity categories," thus "avowing the sign's strategic provisionality (rather than its strategic essentialism)" (1991:14, 19). Despite this call for *non*-absolutist thinking on the part of lesbian writers, many lesbians insist on a kind of lesbian purity test, defining their own lesbianism by excluding bisexuals, transsexuals, and leatherwomen as somehow less lesbian than others. Rather than a tolerance for ambiguity, there is an embrace of exclusivity, with some lesbians insisting on a very narrow definition of the term, condemning sexual practices they do not approve of, and erecting literal admission barriers against women they deem inappropriate (pre-op transsexuals and leatherwomen, in particular) from women's festivals.

As a lesbian, a mother, a tenured professor, and a leatherwoman, I wish, in this essay, to indicate the dangers of binary/exclusionary thinking and the implied lesbian purity test, and I wish to explore the embrace of contraries and ambiguity that bisexuals, transsexuals and leatherwomen embody. As a diverse and heterogenous community, we must question labels, essentialist and absolutist thinking, and binary distinctions. While not all lesbians engage in such exclusionary labelling and stereotyping, the ones who do tend to be very vocal in expressing their opinions and in flatly dismissing any point of view that doesn't conform to their own. In so doing, they insist that some lesbians are more equal than others, suggesting that those lesbians who do not meet their strict definitions do not belong in the same space. I have frequently witnessed such positions being expressed on particular Internet newsgroups and mailing lists designated for lesbians *and* bisexual women, but I am withholding the names of these forums for purposes of confidentiality. Bisexuals on such a newsgroup have been derided by lesbians who say, for instance, that they will never get involved with bi women for fear of being left for a man, as if only bisexuals dump their girlfriends, while lesbians do not.

But what does it mean to be lesbian or bisexual? There are self-defined lesbians who have sex with men, self-defined lesbians who have been aware of their sexuality since childhood, self-defined lesbians who became aware of their sexuality only after a heterosexual marriage, and self-defined lesbians who emphasize their politics and woman-identification more than the gender of their sexual partners. Some self-described bisexuals are women in monogamous heterosexual relationships who also feel attraction to women; some are women who say that gender is irrelevant to their attraction to another person; some are women who are also polyamorous, having relationships with members of both genders; some are previously straight women who discovered an attraction to a woman or women; some are lesbians who discovered an attraction to a man or men. The insistence on single meanings for the terms "lesbian" and "bisexual" ignores the experiences of many people who have a fluid or changing sexual identity. Paula C. Rust posits that "sexual identity is more usefully understood as a representation of one's location on the sexual landscape, a location that is described in terms of one's relationship to other people, groups, and institutions on that landscape." As such, "sexual identity is thus not a static representation of essential being but a dynamic description of the self in relation to others" (1996:77-78). As Rust notes, "bisexuality is often categorized as a challenge to gendered categories and to dualistic binary thinking in general" (1996:80). Thus, bisexuality is often perceived as a threat, yet "monosexual identities are challenged by the dynamic nature of sexual identity; they are unstable and require constant defense and repair even without the threat of a bisexual identity" (1996:80). Such lesbians seem to fear that any acknowledgement of the dynamic nature of sexual identities will undermine the lesbian movement.

The implied purity test that some lesbians apply to women who don't meet their criteria–as in the case of a poster on an Internet newsgroup who insisted that only "100% true-blue lesbians" were entitled to sport Pride stickers on their cars–becomes even more pronounced when it comes to the definition of "woman." Pre-operative male-to-female transsexuals are excluded as a matter of policy from the Michigan Women's Music Festival, among other women's events. They are also a target of hostility on lesbian and bisexual Internet forums. One poster on such a mailing list told a transsexual member that she did not belong there, as she is not a woman, but a man "role-playing" a woman. Thus, a privileging of "womyn-born-womyn" takes place, as one lengthy newsgroup thread reveals. Such a conception naively equates gender with anatomy and throws up a defensive wall against "undesirable" elements by claiming the sanctity of a safe "woman-only" space with no dicks allowed. By contrast, listening to and reading the experiences of transsexuals might allow us to conceive of gender in broader, less rigid terms. Are gender, identity, and anatomy all to be conflated, thus excluding transsexual women from our community, or can we begin to think of gender in less absolute and binary ways?

The same absolutist and binary thinking that excludes bisexuals and transsexuals from the lesbian community is even more prominent in discussions of bdsm. (The acronym "bdsm" covers a fuller spectrum of kinky activities than "s/m" does: discipline and bondage, dominance and submission, sadism and masochism.) Again, some lesbian feminists apply a kind of purity test to sexual practices, arguing that certain activities are not acceptable and are anti-feminist. For example, the typical and repeated claims in the book *Against Sadomasochism* (henceforth *AS/m*), edited by Linden, Pagano, Russell and Star (1982), are as follows: (1) "lesbian sadomasochism is firmly rooted in patriarchal sexual ideology" (Linden, 1992:4); (2) sexual behavior and relationships are socially constructed, which makes consent irrelevant to sadomasochistic relationships; (3) sadomasochism imitates a heterosexual model of male power over women; (4) practicing sadomasochism perpetuates women's oppression and "the values of the patriarchal ruling class" (Meredith, 1982:97) and validates "the system in which one person has power over another, which is the basis of patriarchy" (Wagner, 1982:34); and (5) consensual sadomasochism is indistinguishable from abuse. Such arguments are made by other authors as well. A much more recent book, Claudia Card's *Lesbian Choices*, speculates that sadomasochism may undermine "resistance to oppression by eroticizing domination and subordinance" (1995:236) and "may purge us of revolutionary impulses, not only by getting rid of our hostilities but also by redirecting them, channelling them ultimately against ourselves and those who should be our allies" (1995:237). I wish to indicate some of the flaws in such simplistic arguments before going on to discuss the ways in which bdsm can be an exploration and celebration of ambiguity and contraries.

The authors in *AS/m*, among others, describe women as prisoners of an ideology of male dominance and violence and female submission and passivity. They make a simplistic and deterministic equation between the personal and political, attempting to analyze the social construction of relationships, yet their "analyses" are often so strident, one must wonder just what these authors are so afraid of? The persistent equation of consensual s/m to abuse and battering sounds suspiciously like the right-wing's equation of homosexuality with pedophilia. It's not to say that abuse doesn't ever take place in bdsm relationships or that pedophiles who prefer same-sex victims don't exist; but in both cases an entire community is adjudged guilty because of the crimes of a few members, without acknowledging that abuse takes place in vanilla (i.e., non-kinky) relation-ships as well, and not all pedophiles pursue victims of the same sex.

In their focus on the social construction of sexuality, the authors in *AS/m* deny that women engaging in bdsm can consent meaningfully or make a free choice; such women are somehow both unthinking victims and violent perpetuators of patriarchal ideology. They're not so much arguing that women are incapable of choice; instead, they argue that women who participate in bdsm are not capable of choice, while women who engage in "egalitarian" relationships with other women are. John Stoltenberg, for example, goes so far as to claim that "between two homo-sexual males . . . there exists the possibility that 'consent' in sadomasoch-ism may be meaningful: its meaning is in their prior agreement as phallic peers to reify each other's manhood" (1982:127). Only "genital males" can "act willfully and without constraint" in our culture; thus, "the woman's compliance or acquiescence in sadomasochism is therefore en-tirely delusional and utterly meaningless" (1982:128). As a feminist and an active practitioner of bdsm, I find such arguments both patronizing and mindlessly absolutist. As Patricia L. Duncan points out, such claims do not allow women the status of subject (1996:102). Or, I might add, they only allow women the status of free agent or subject if they make the proper, politically correct choices–that is, relationships free of dominance and submission. In their *AS/m* article, Jeanette Nichols, Darlene Pagano and Margaret Rossoff claim, "What looks like free choice is often forced upon people by education, the media and other cultural institutions" (1982:137). Yet, an individual's response to media and culture is hardly a simple cause and effect. The mirroring relationship between the audience and popular culture goes both ways. In addition, people are not inevitably brainwashed by the media; many are very capable of analyzing and assess-ing the messages our culture promotes. To acknowledge the influence of culture on an individual does not have to deny that individual any agency in her response to that culture. In my experience, the women I know in the leather community are not ignorant, mindless clones, unwittingly acting out a patriarchal, oppressive ideology. Their entrance into the active prac-tice of bdsm is a result of conscious questioning, struggle, deliberation, and choice. As Duncan points out, the participants in her study "were extremely knowledgeable about current theoretical discourses concerning feminism, sexuality, and power" (1996:90). The same goes in my experi-ence. For instance, a current example of the intersection between feminism and bdsm is occurring within the National Organization for Women. A group of **NOW** members are working to reform NOW's policy statement on s/m. They are very aware of feminist arguments against s/m, yet they have concluded that their sexuality and their feminism are not mutually exclusive. Women who practice bdsm are also aware that they are not solely defined by their sexuality. A submissive masochist can be a competent professional; a dominant sadist can be a loving parent. We are not exclusively determined by our preferred sexual roles. We can fight oppressive power in the outside world and play with erotic power in the bedroom, and we can do our jobs and nurture our children, realizing that who we are is not confined to a single label.

The authors of *AS/m* make repeated equations that are evidence of dualistic thinking: masochism with passivity, sadism with abuse, power with oppression, submission with victimhood. Like Card, they equate what goes on in the bedroom with political attitudes in the outside world. A particularly egregious list of equations is made in Susan Griffin's essay, in which she equates the roles of "the Nazi to the Jew," and "the white master to the black slave" with "professor to student" and "parent to child" (1982:185). As both a professor and a parent, I hardly see those roles as inherently oppressive. To equate the roles of professor and parent to Nazi and slave-master is absurd, and a typical example of the type of either/or binary thinking that pervades *AS/m*. I wish to posit, by contrast, that bdsm is a form of play with opposites. It is an exploration of the ambiguity at the essence of human existence. The first point to be made is that bdsm does not involve the unconscious adoption of oppressive, patriarchal, and heterosexual roles. The roles adopted in a scene are, as Duncan points out, "constructed and negotiated" (1996:99). As she notes, "In s/m play, identities are not stable, static, or even necessarily clearly demarcated; rather, they are constructed, imaginary, and constantly shifting" (1996:88). Marissa Jonel, in *AS/m*, states, "I never met a 'top' that wasn't a sadist nor a 'bottom' that wasn't a masochist" (1982:17). All I can say is that her experience must have been very limited. There are dominant masochists and submissive sadists. There are masochists who have no interest in submission and submissives who have no interest in pain. There are sadists who are interested only in creating sensation, not dominating, and there are dominants who are not interested in inflicting pain. There are many "switches" who actively embrace both top and bottom roles. The roles may or may not extend out of the bedroom. In my own case I am both a control freak and a submissive masochist. In my professional life I am competent, organized, assertive, in control, and highly resistant to authority. I am anti-authoritarian in my political leanings as well. As a control freak, I find the ability to surrender control to another, in a safe space, extremely liberating. In *AS/m*, Karen Rian describes submission as "self-diminution" (1982:48). On the contrary, many submissives describe the experience as empowering and fulfilling, a discovery of their own strength and courage. My wife often jokes that she's the sadist because she's a wimp. Far from it, but it takes a certain kind of strength to surrender one's trappings of power from the outside world and to serve and submit with pride. By the same token, the sadist who acknowledges and accepts her sadism makes herself vulnerable by revealing her desires. The strength and vulnerability are located in both roles. Anti-s/m crusaders insist that the bottom is inevitably a victim of patriarchy, reenacting that victimization in the bedroom. Yet, another possibility exists. Perhaps the bottom who has proved her own strength and power during an intense flogging can call on that same strength and power when she needs it in the outside world. It is not unusual for the submissive partner in a bdsm relationship to be assertive and self-responsible in the other aspects of her life.

Anti-s/m feminists equate power with oppression. I think it is possible to look at it another way. Power is a form of energy, structured energy. It can be used and misused. Political power can be used to oppress groups of people, but it can also be used to liberate people from poverty, for instance. Power is not necessarily good or bad. The partners in an s/m scene consciously play with power, exploring its dimensions and exchanging energies to produce what can be a transcendent level of intimacy and intensity. Yet the process is very deliberate, controlled, and stylized, often involving extensive preparation, staging, and negotiation. Many s/m scenes depend heavily on props, costumes, music, candles, and other trappings to create a ritual space or circle, clearly demarcated from the outside world, just as a religious ritual creates a similar type of space. (Ritual is not only a part of s/m; s/m can also be a part of ritual in some spiritual practices.) The collar and cuffs worn by the bottom do not negate her power or oppress her in the outside world; rather, they serve symbolically to demarcate her role in the scene, to channel her energy. By the same token, the sadist's whip becomes an extension of her energy within the ritual space of the scene. It is a conveyor of power, but it is also a conveyor of the top's love, affection, and concern for the bottom. Many sadists appropriately describe themselves as caring; they are anxious to satisfy their bottom, to avoid injuring her physically or psychologically, and to create a space where the bottom can safely fulfill her desire to surrender control. Similarly, masochists often describe the "caress" or "kiss" of the whip, which can express the top's tenderness as much as a literal caress or kiss can.

Humans have a dark side; that is why we are fascinated by violence and crime, pain and power, whether actual or fictional. Most people who watch violent movies or read violent pornography do not go out and start enforcing justice with a high-powered automatic weapon or engaging in rape in the real world. As Rebecca Dawn Kaplan points out, "Playing Monopoly is not the same thing as actually trying to bankrupt everyone and take over the world. An s/m scene is not the same thing as assault" (1996:126). Most people are capable of distinguishing between fantasy and real life, using fantasy to explore their own dark sides without causing injury to others. Some people must risk themselves in order to explore this fascination and engage in extreme sports and death-defying activities such as sky-diving to channel the energy of their dark sides. Those of us who engage in bdsm explore our dark sides in another fashion. We use ritual, symbol, and the exchange of energy in the form of power to transmute the darkness of our deepest desires–to submit, to dominate, to be humiliated, to degrade, to receive pain, to inflict pain–into something else: joy, intimacy, sacredness and a deeply spiritual transcendence of Selfhood. Some liken a scene to a journey or quest, in which both partners work together toward a common goal. As Pat Califia suggests, "People choose to endure pain or discomfort if the goal they are striving for makes it worthwhile. Long-distance runners are not generally thought of as sex perverts, nor is St. Theresa" (1996:234). Pain can be a vehicle to achieve a heightened state of awareness or a state of oneness with one's partner and the universe or, simply, a blissful endorphin high.

Thus, the notion of the bottom's victimhood and passivity and the comparison of the bottom's role with the traditional female role are false. Scenes between new acquaintances are often preceded by a period of formal negotiation, both parties specifying what they like, what they don't like, and what they may be willing to try. Checklists of activities, ranging from fisting to flogging, circulate on the Internet and are printed in books and can be used as part of the negotiation. The bottom is given a verbal or non-verbal safeword so she can call a break in or a halt to a scene. Mailing lists, newsgroups and other forums exist to exchange information on how to perform various procedures in a safe manner, and safety is emphasized in books on the subject and in convention workshops. It is possible that kinky couples engage in more extensive communication about sexual needs, desires, and dislikes than vanilla couples do because the mechanism for such communication is so ingrained in the bdsm community, the members of which go out of their way to gather information from a variety of sources. Tops are expected to monitor the bottom's condition and to provide any necessary aftercare. The bottom is hardly a passive victim, but rather an active participant in achieving the sexual experience she desires. Despite the exchange of power and the top's overt control, there is truth to the cliché that the person who has the real control is the bottom.

This is not to say there is no danger, no risk. Flirting with physical danger is part of the thrill, just as it is for extreme athletes. There is also the psychological risk that a scene may set off an emotional trigger. In both cases, the participants weigh the desired intimacy and intensity against the possible risks. Those elements of danger and vulnerability put both parties in a heightened mental state, and the trust involved allows for a highly intimate connection to take place. The controlled and consensual violence of a scene can have a purifying effect, allowing both participants to shed social roles and trappings and touch each other on a primal level. In such a case, the violence and closeness are one and the same thing.

Crusaders against bdsm contrast "egalitarian" or "equal" relationships to relationships based on dominance and submission. A more complex point of view, however, would envision a radical equality involved in the consensual exchange of power. At its best, in bdsm, both parties are getting exactly what they want while mutually satisfying their partner. Both parties give pleasure to each other and receive pleasure from each other. Both parties accept and nourish the other's needs and desires without judgment or condemnation. Contrary to what an outsider might expect, the women's kinky community, in fact, tends to be tolerant, open-minded, and accepting of individual differences. Some tops are femmes, some tops are daddies (and some daddies can be femmes); some bottoms are butch boys, some bottoms are femmes. The participants are aware that they are playing with roles and engaging in genderfuck; bdsm roles are hardly a slavish and mindless recreation of heterosexuality. Diane Richardson asserts that "we could see the recent emergence of lesbian porn and erotica, with its privileging of certain kinds of activities, as a pressure to accept as the norm for lesbian sex sexual values which have previously been associated with heterosexuality" (1996:285). Isn't it possible that lesbian porn and erotica exist to explore fantasies of the author and readers, not as a means to "pressure" other lesbians to adopt the same "sexual values?" Isn't it possible that porn and erotica and the practice of bdsm in real life can be a deliberate and consciously chosen form of play, not a recreation of heterosexual values? To insist that power is exclusively masculine, as anti-s/m writers do, strikes me as a depressingly pessimistic viewpoint, one that implies that feminism has had no impact on society and that women are incapable of achieving any kind of autonomy, agency, or power whatsoever.

A recent and particularly blatant example of the simplistic and dualistic thinking of anti-s/m crusaders is Sheila Jeffreys' *The Lesbian Heresy*. She rehashes all the old arguments that s/m is a reenactment of "our very real oppression" (1993:174) and "the heterosexual system of male dominance and female submission" (1993:179); that it "glorifies and legitimates violence" (1993:188); that consent is a "male supremacist" model of sexuality in which "one person, generally male, uses the body of another who is not necessarily interested and possibly generally reluctant or distressed, as a sex aid" (1993:39); that it is a form of "internalised anti-lesbianism and self-hatred" (1993:188); and a way to "justify politically oppressive systems, i.e., the basic fascist value that the masses 'need' a strong ruler" (1993:189). Again for Jeffreys, power and sexual desire are purely masculine traits, and "consent is a tool for negotiating inequality in heterosexual relations" (1993:39). Quite apart from the fact that she never considers that some heterosexual women might *enjoy* sex–they are either uninterested or "reluctant or distressed," or if they enjoy it they've been brainwashed by the image of the passive, submissive female–Jeffreys doesn't acknowledge that the bottom in a bdsm encounter is hardly being used "as a sex aid." It is the bottom, after all, who is the recipient of all those glorious sensations she actively seeks out; as a bottom myself, I feel quite grateful for the all the work my wife does to give me pleasure. Of course, the pleasure is mutual, and consensuality is a mechanism to ensure that it stays that way. While Jeffreys' notion of consent may very well apply to some relationships, it doesn't even come close to the reality of mutual, consensual, freely chosen bdsm. This is not surprising, as she sees s/m as a "form of self-injury" in which "another person performs the injury but at the behest of the self-mutilator" (1993:35). Quite apart from the fact that she provides no support for this psychological insight, it seems to contradict the notion that it is the top who is in the masculine and dominant role and bottom merely a passive recipient who "consents" to be injured. Here, she seems to suggest that the bottom manipulates the top into orchestrating her own self-mutilation.

It is not only overt s/m that enacts "the heterosexual system of male dominance and female submission" (1993:179), according to Jeffreys, but dildos do as well. In an astonishingly poor argument, Jeffreys asserts that "like the penis," dildos "symbolize male power and the ability to violate women" (1993:28). She associates them with s/m, where of course they are used, without acknowledging that a great many vanilla lesbians incorporate dildos into their sex life without any overtones of dominance and submission. She announces that the "dildo allows for the slavish imitation of heterosexual sex," since a dildo is "an imitation penis" (1993:29). My only question to Jeffreys is, if a dildo is an imitation penis, and penetrative sex an imitation of heterosexual sex, why aren't lesbians leaving their female partners in search of the "real thing" with a man? It doesn't occur to her that sex with a dildo is geared very much toward the pleasure of the bottom, unlike heterosexual sex which has its climax in the male's ejaculation. Dildos come in interesting shapes, sizes, or colors (many of which are nowhere near anatomically correct), don't go limp, and don't need stimulation. They seem to me a particularly woman-centered sex toy. Yet, in her distress about the use of these imitation penises, Jeffreys laments, "What is astonishing is the lack of a widespread lesbian revolt against the incursion of the dildo, a symbol of male power and the oppression of women, into lesbian culture" (1993:30). What is astonishing to me is that Jeffreys actually expects lesbians to "revolt" against a sex toy, an instrument of pleasure, and utterly fails to understand why more lesbians don't share her views. She argues that "the lesbian pornographers and sex industrialists are telling us that lesbians are disadvantaged by the absence of a penis" (1993:30), yet I would counter her argument with the oft-repeated joke that lesbians don't have penis envy because they have drawers full of them. I suspect that many lesbians with a decent sex life think it is men who are disadvantaged by their anatomy; it's all a matter of perspective, but perspective is a quality Jeffreys sorely lacks.

This lack of perspective is revealed in Jeffreys' statement of her thesis, "that pornography, sadomasochism and roleplaying are hostile to the lesbian feminist project" (1993:xi). Her assumption that there is one, monolithic "lesbian feminist project" and that anything that deviates from her brand of lesbian feminism is, by definition, anti-feminist overshadows the entire book, invalidating her arguments from the start. In a recent discussion of feminism on a leatherwoman's Internet mailing list, several members proclaimed their feminism with pride, with one poster, Damion Kelley, noting, "I didn't join a women's liberation movement to replace one 'List of Things I'm Not Allowed To Do Because I'm a Woman' with another 'List of Things I'm Not Allowed To Do Because I'm a Woman.'"

Jeffreys' most significant argument against s/m is her discussion of connections between s/m and fascism and the use of fascist symbols in s/m scenes. I believe I've already countered the argument that the practice of s/m renders women more likely to eroticize political power and less likely to fight oppression. That is simply unsupported with a shred of evidence and untrue; many practitioners of s/m are politically active in women's and glbt causes as well as other fights against oppressive political systems. Thus, Jeffreys cannot support her claim that "only the building of an egalitarian sexual practice can fit into anti-fascist politics" (1993:187). Fascism is a form of institutionalized authority imposed on an unwilling group of people; the power of the top in an s/m scene is wholly different, freely granted by the bottom for the duration of the scene to further an exchange of energy that is mutually pleasurable and beneficial. Jeffreys is comparing apples and oranges. As Rebecca Dawn Kaplan asserts, "rather than argue that power play is okay because I don't care about politics, I want to argue that women's right to sexual pleasure, exploration, and self-determination is political, is feminist, and is a positive act" (1996:129). Where Jeffreys' argument has some validity is in the condemnation of fascist symbols used by some members of the s/m community. Like many other practioners of s/m, I am also horrified by the use of swastikas and Nazi uniforms in s/m play. I am not alone. The editors of *The Second Coming*, a recent follow-up to Samois' *Coming to Power*, chose to include an essay that explicitly condemns the use of such symbols. Linda Wayne argues:

> Practitioners of s/m or members of any other subgroup who choose to adopt a historically accurate symbol such as the swastika are representing themselves in a way that is continuous with the dominant imagery and state-level ideological interests of Third Reich Nazism. Even when the individuals claim that they are merely playing with such symbols, they are responsible for choosing a "plaything" that has been recuperated within the living symbolism of current neo-Nazi subgroups. (1996:249)

What Wayne's essay reveals, and what Jeffreys utterly fails to acknowledge, is that practitioners of bdsm aren't any more a homogenous monolithic group than lesbian feminists are. Some members of the leather community engage in activities that are soundly condemned by other members of the same community. As Pat Califia's essay in *The Second Coming* (1996) reveals, some members of the community are working to eradicate nonconsensual abuse within the community. Members of the leather community vehemently debate the safety of various sexual and s/m practices. Some members of the s/m dyke community welcome allegiances with gay men and with straight practioners of s/m; others insist on women-only spaces. Not all s/m dykes are abusers or abused; not all s/m dykes use Nazi symbols in their scenes.

Jeffreys' generalizations about the practice of s/m partake of the same types of group stereotyping that "phobes" use against gays and lesbians. This is also true of other anti-s/m crusaders. As Kaplan suggests, "one of the reasons we attack each other with such virulence is that we can. Other dykes are safer targets than those with more power" (1996:129). She notes, further, "while we tear at each other, those who would be happy to see all 'outlaws' eliminated are continuing their work unimpeded" (1996:130). Jeffreys' analysis of the reasons for our eroticization of power and powerlessness may be partially correct: "western male supremacy encourages us to experience sexuality as an immensely powerful and nigh uncontrollable force" (1993:179). Yet she goes on to associate the practice of s/m with lesbian self-hatred that arises from heterosexism. The first claim acknowledges the role social construction plays in our sexuality, yet the second claim, like so much of her analysis, lacks any concrete evidence. I won't deny that politics, media, and popular culture have a hand in shaping our sexual predilections. But neither will I argue that women are innately good and pure and have been warped entirely by the cultures in which they live. We do have a dark side, we do have violent urges. S/m allows for the eroticization of power and powerlessness to be transformed, controlled and channelled through negotiations and the mechanism of consent, through the dissemination of information about safety throughout the leather community, and through the structured ritual elements of a scene into an expression of love, intimacy, and mutual caring. The scene space becomes a sacred circle where contraries do exist: pain becomes pleasure, control becomes freedom, and darkness becomes light.

It is, apparently, the embrace of contraries and ambiguity that biphobes, transphobes, and anti-s/m crusaders seem to find threatening. It is disturbing to me, although not entirely unexpected, that members of a marginalized community would practice the same type of exclusion practiced against them by homophobic and anti-feminist oppressors. Such ideological rigidity and the insistence on binary oppositions by some lesbians, particularly radical separatists such as Jeffreys, may result from a fear that lesbian feminism will be undermined or even eradicated if it is diluted by impure, "politically incorrect" elements. Or the fear may be even more basic; like virulent homophobes, the lesbians who insist on a kind of purity test may simply be afraid of those who are different from themselves. I would argue, by contrast, that the lesbian feminist movement is strengthened by diversity and by the acknowledgment and awareness that there is more than one way to be a lesbian and a feminist.

REFERENCES

Anzaldúa, Gloria. *Borderlands/La Frontera: The New Mestiza*. San Francisco: Aunt Lute Books, 1987.

Butler, Judith. "Imitation and Gender Insubordination." In *Inside/Out: Lesbian Theories, Gay Theories*. Ed. Diana Fuss. NY, London: Routledge, 1991, 13-31.

Califia, Pat. "A House Divided: Violence in the Lesbian S/M Community." In *The Second Coming: A Leatherdyke Reader*. Eds. Pat Califia and Robin Sweeney. Los Angeles: Alyson Publications, 1996, 264-274.

_____. "Feminism and Sadomasochism." In *Feminism and Sexuality: A Reader*. Eds. Stevi Jackson and Sue Scott. NY: Columbia UP, 1996, 230-237.

Card, Claudia. *Lesbian Choices*. NY: Columbia UP, 1995.

Duncan, Patricia L. "Identity, Power, and Difference: Negotiating Conflict in an S/M Dyke Community." In *Queer Studies: A Lesbian, Gay, Bisexual & Transgender Anthology*. Eds. Brett Beemyn and Mickey Eliason. NY, London: New York UP, 1996, 87-114.

Griffin, Susan. "Sadomasochism and the Erosion of Self: A Critical Reading of Story of O." In *Against Sadomasochism: A Radical Feminist Analysis*. Eds. Robin Ruth Linden, Diana E. H. Russell, and Susan Leigh Star. East Palo Alto, CA: Frog in the Well, 1982, 184-201.

Jeffreys, Sheila. *The Lesbian Heresy: A Feminist Perspective on the Lesbian Sexual Revolution*. North Melbourne, Australia: Spinifex Press, 1993.

Jonel, Marisa. "Letter from a Former Masochist." In *Against Sadomasochism: A Radical Feminist Analysis*. Eds. Robin Ruth Linden, Darlene Pagano, Diana E. H. Russell, and Susan Leigh Star. East Palo Alto, CA: Frog in the Well, 1982, 16-22.

Kaplan, Rebecca Dawn. "Sex, Lies, and Heteropatriarchy: The S/M Debates at the Michigan Womyn's Music Festival." In *The Second Coming: A Leatherdyke Reader*. Eds. Pat Califia and Robin Sweeney. Los Angeles: Alyson Publications, 1996, 123-130.

Linden, Robin Ruth. "Introduction: Against Sadomasochism." In *Against Sadomasochism: A Radical Feminist Analysis*. Eds. Robin Ruth Linden, Darlene Pagano, Diana E. H. Russell, and Susan Leigh Star. East Palo Alto, CA: Frog in the Well, 1982, 1-15.

Linden, Robin Ruth, Darlene R. Pagano, Diana E. H. Russell, and Susan Leigh Star, eds. *Against Sadomasochism: A Radical Feminist Analysis*. East Palo Alto, CA: Frog in the Well, 1982.

Meredith, Jesse. "A Response to Samois." In *Against Sadomasochism: A Radical Feminist Analysis*. Eds. Robin Ruth Linden, Darlene Pagano, Diana E. H. Russell, and Susan Leigh Star. East Palo Alto, CA: Frog in the Well, 1982, 96-98.

Nichols, Jeanette, Darlene Pagano, and Margaret Rossoff. "Is Sadomasochism Feminist? A Critique of the Samois Position." In *Against Sadomasochism: A Radical Feminist Analysis*. Eds. Robin Ruth Linden, Darlene Pagano, Diana E. H. Russell, and Susan Leigh Star. East Palo Alto, CA: Frog in the Well, 1982, 137-146.

NOW S/M Policy Reform Project. Web site: http://members.aol.com/NOWSM/Home.html.

Rian, Karen. "Sadomasochism and the Social Construction of Desire." In *Against Sadomasochism: A Radical Feminist Analysis*. Eds. Robin Ruth Linden, Darlene Pagano, Diana E. H. Russell, and Susan Leigh Star. East Palo Alto, CA: Frog in the Well, 1982, 45-50.

Richardson, Diane. "Constructing Lesbian Sexualities." In *Feminism and Sexuality: A Reader*. Eds. Stevi Jackson and Sue Scott. NY: Columbia UP, 1996, 276-287.

Rust, Paula C. "Sexual Identity and Bisexual Indentities: The Struggle for Self-

Description in a Changing Sexual Landscape." In *Queer Studies: A Lesbian, Gay, Bisexual & Transgender Anthology.* Eds. Brett Beemyn and Mickey Eliason. NY, London: New York UP, 1996, 64-86.

Stoltenberg, John. "Sadomasochism: Eroticized Violence, Eroticized Powerlessness." In *Against Sadomasochism: A Radical Feminist Analysis.* Eds. Robin Ruth Linden, Darlene Pagano, Diana E. H. Russell, and Susan Leigh Star. East Palo Alto, CA: Frog in the Well, 1982, 124-130.

Wagner, Sally Roesch. "Pornography and the Sexual Revolution: The Backlash of Sadomasochism." In *Against Sadomasochism: A Radical Feminist Analysis.* Eds. Robin Ruth Linden, Darlene Pagano, Diana E. H. Russell, and Susan Leigh Star. East Palo Alto, CA: Frog in the Well, 1982, 242-251.

Wayne, Linda. "S/M Symbols, Fascist Icons, and Systems of Empowerment." In *The Second Coming: A Leatherdyke Reader.* Eds. Pat Califia and Robin Sweeney. Los Angeles: Alyson Publications, 1996, 23-44.

Wittig, Monique. *The Lesbian Body.* Tr. David Le Fay. Boston: Beacon Press, 1986.

Gender Role Reversal
and the Violated Lesbian Body:
Toward a Feminist Hermeneutic
of Lesbian Sadomasochism

Teresa J. Hornsby

SUMMARY. The lesbian sadomasochist exists in the feminist community as doubly other. If she is addressed at all in feminist discourses, she is often accused of wielding the weapons of patriarchy (violence, danger, fear) against all that feminism is. In what follows I will construct a theoretical framework which suggests that lesbian sadomasochism is not antithetical to feminism. In fact, lesbian sadomasochism is, on numerous levels, a response to those things deemed damaging to women. *[Article copies available for a fee from The Haworth Document Delivery Service: 1-800-342-9678. E-mail address: getinfo@haworthpressinc.com]*

INTRODUCTION

Above the din of the debates about women's sexuality, the lived experience of the sadomasochist woman remains: she finds value, whether per-

Teresa Hornsby is a doctoral candidate in New Testament at Vanderbilt University. She received a BS from the University of Tennessee and an MTS from Harvard Divinity School. Her dissertation, "Re-Reading Women's Transgression in the Gospel of Luke" is in progress.

Address correspondence to: Teresa J. Hornsby, Vanderbilt University, The Divinity School, Nashville, TN 37240.

[Haworth co-indexing entry note]: "Gender Role Reversal and the Violated Lesbian Body: Toward a Feminist Hermeneutic of Lesbian Sadomasochism." Hornsby, Teresa J. Co-published simultaneously in *Journal of Lesbian Studies* (The Haworth Press, Inc.) Vol. 3, No. 3, 1999, pp. 61-72; and: *Lesbian Sex Scandals: Sexual Practices, Identities, and Politics* (ed: Dawn Atkins) The Haworth Press, Inc., 1999, pp. 61-72; and: *Lesbian Sex Scandals: Sexual Practices, Identities, and Politics* (ed: Dawn Atkins) Harrington Park Press, an imprint of The Haworth Press, Inc., 1999, pp. 61-72. Single or multiple copies of this article are available for a fee from The Haworth Document Delivery Service [1-800-342-9678, 9:00 a.m. - 5:00 p.m. (EST). E-mail address: getinfo@haworthpressinc.com].

sonal, whether political, in the violent infliction or passive acceptance of pain and humiliation in her erotic life. How, then, can one dismiss depictions and practice of SM that some women find transformative and liberative? Conversely, how can these images be made accessible for some without perpetuating violence and degradation to others? I will not even pretend I can answer these questions. But I am convinced that women who self-identify as sadists and masochists would not automatically see themselves and what they do as counter to feminism. In fact, I will argue not only that SM is not antithetical to the concerns of feminism, but also that it can be a particular and powerful articulation of feminist theory.

My purpose is to examine several theoretical frameworks possible for the interpretation of lesbian SM and to suggest directions for further consideration of how SM women may find representation in, rather than derision from, the feminist movement. I am primarily interested in the social and religious implications of SM theory. I will focus on lesbian SM for two main reasons: lesbian SMists are targeted with exceptionally harsh criticism from some radical feminists, perhaps because some factions believe lesbians to be representative of a "feminine" sexuality that exists already outside a phallocentric framework. For example, Rosemary Tong writes, "At first, many radical feminists believed that in order to be liberated, women must escape the confines of heterosexuality and create an exclusively female sexuality through celibacy, autoeroticism, or lesbianism" (1989:5). Some radical feminists believe that SM compromises this identity and that SM lesbians replicate the abuses of patriarchy. To these critics, there is a strict dichotomous relationship between feminism and SM. Another reason I am focusing on lesbian SM is because I believe it to be particularly transgressive and, in some ways, unique. Lesbian SM incorporates (makes corporeal) the excesses of the taboo. Further, some psychoanalytical feminists have suggested the lesbian sadomasochist exists within a completely alternative sexual frame.

My method for this paper will remain entirely theoretical. While I think most future work on lesbian SM should deal directly with the stories of the women themselves, this paper is merely a rudimentary step toward instilling SM into a feminist discourse. I will make strong use of the theories of Georges Bataille, Mary Douglas, Rene Girard and Judith Butler to come to my own conclusions concerning the feminist value of patriarchal subversion in lesbian SM. The offerings of Bataille on the inter-relatedness of sexuality, taboo and the sacred are particularly cogent for pulling together the seemingly antithetical relationship of violence and the erotic or, rather, Thanatos and Eros. Two aspects in the work of Girard also strongly influence this paper. First, the victim (in SM, the masochist) is the point of intersection between the profane and the sacred. Second, Girard identifies a necessary, sanctioned violence. I will explore the implications of a "positive" violence in a lesbian SM context. Butler's framework of the subversive nature of gender role-reversal and gender role parody provides another dimension to role-playing within lesbian SM scenes. Finally, Douglas's work, which I will use cooperatively with Butler's, also complements Bataille in its positioning of the body and the boundaries of the body as symbolic of cultures and the boundaries of cultures. It is through the conflation of Butler's and Douglas's work that I will be able to talk about what a violated lesbian body means in the context of reversed gender roles. Ultimately, in this paper I am working toward an understanding of lesbian SM that moves it out of its spurious designation as destructive, phallocentrically defined, violence against women.

SADOMASOCHISM: A BRIEF HISTORY OF INTERPRETATION

The question "Why are women sadomasochist?" has several answers. According to Carol Truscott, there are four main reasons: "the endorphin high, the spiritual experience, the individual psychological benefit, and pure play" (1991:21). The prominent feminist discourses, from liberal feminism to radical feminism, have not really confronted the value and pleasure that SM represents in many women's lives, particularly lesbian women. Many feminists observe the violence, pain and humiliation involved in SM play and reject it because they believe there is no value at all in these experiences; because violence particularly is something created by a patriarchal system; or because it is something inherently evil and can neither be movement toward wholeness nor toward the sacred (see Hopkins, 1994:116-141). For example, Andrea Dworkin's underlying implication throughout her work is that SM replicates patriarchal interactions thus perpetuating and validating patriarchal and hegemonic power. Rather, I would suggest along with Patrick Hopkins that there is a difference between the replication of hegemonic power relationships and the simulation of them.

Hopkins writes, "Replication implies that SM encounters merely reproduce patriarchal activity in a different physical area. Simulation implies that SM selectively replays surface patriarchal behaviors onto a different contextual field. That contextual field makes a profound difference" (1994:123). Though the SM play may look extremely real, there are immense differences between, for example, a real rape and a staged rape, or a stabbing and a blood letting. The primary distinction is consent: there is negotiation, there are safe words, and there is predetermined mutual agreement about what will and will not happen. I find the following metaphor of a woman in a roller coaster very helpful in understanding the difference between replication and simulation concerning women and SM:

> In significant ways, SM scenes parallel the experience of being on a roller coaster. There is intense emotion—fear, tension, anticipation, thrill. There is a physiological arousal—adrenaline rush, headiness, gut twisting, a body high. All this because one has placed herself in the position of simulating plummeting to her death, of simulating flying off into space, of simulating the possibility of smashing into trees or metal railings. But is the best interpretation of the roller coaster rider's desire that she really would like to plummet to her death or collide with another train? Is it the case that she genuinely desires to be crushed against the ground, but because the law and conventional morality attempt to prevent it, alas, she is not able? Is riding a roller coaster just a matter of settling for the weaker imitation, for the copy of plummeting to her death?
>
> Of course not. In fact, the experience desired by the roller coaster rider is precisely the simulation of those lethal experiences—not because simulation is all she can get, but because the simulation itself is thrilling and satisfying. So in the same way the roller coaster rider may find actually falling to her death repugnant and horrible, but finds simulation of that event thrilling and exciting, the SM practitioner may find actual violence and humiliation repugnant and horrible, but finds the simulation of that event thrilling and exciting—not as a stand-in but as a goal in itself. (Hopkins, 1994:125-6)

Still, with all the attempts at explanation, public apologetics, or theorization of SM, the gulf between the repulsion experienced by some women toward SM and the desire of others is ever widening. Thus, the debate within feminism still rages on and cannot be without casualties.

THE SACRED AND THE THEORY OF RELIGION IN BATAILLE

Bataille, who has influenced the work of Derrida, Foucault, and Irigaray, provides an insightful ingress into practices that are traditionally portrayed as difficult and disturbing. Though I will concentrate on the ideas of Bataille that concern violence, the erotic and their connectedness to the Sacred, I will focus specifically on the theories about sacrifice, eroticism and the dialectic between taboo and transgression. I will suggest that through the practice of SM sex, lesbians, as both sadists and masochists, utilize the images of excess, such as incest, certain gender role reversals, and subversions of traditional power regimes, to manipulate the dialectic between transgression and the taboo.

In order to bring Bataille into a feminist composition, one should make some brief remarks regarding his sexist, heterosexist and misogynist language. While I acknowledge Bataille's disregard for women, his assumption of male dominance and his narrow-minded persistence of heterosexual norms, the essence of his work lies in his awareness of a dark eroticism connected with the Sacred. Bataille sensed that transgression, sinning, if you will, is not only necessary to hold society in balance but also necessary to encounter the Sacred.

Bataille's theory of religion is shaped primarily by stressing transgression, otherness and excess (Olson, 1994:231-250). The sacred for Bataille is complete, chaotic Otherness. Bataille would agree with Douglas, Turner, and others that taboos set up strict definitions between the world and the sacred. However, the chaos fostered by transgression is a part of the sacred rather than antithetical to it. The essence of the sacred opposes the world of order and work. Douglas writes, "It is only by exaggerating the difference between within and without, above and below, male and female, with and against, that a semblance of order is created" (1966:4). In Douglas' work, that "semblance of order" is representative of the sacred. In Bataille, the "order" is antonymous to the sacred.

The sacred for Bataille encompasses all those categories that resist dialectic classification, those that stand apart and threaten to break down rigid lines of definition, particularly the interiors of the body, e.g., excrement, semen, menstrual blood. The sacred should evoke in us feelings of terror because it is always on the edge of erupting into violence (Bataille, 1989:52). And the terror that humans feel is further prompted by the idea that it is a contagious violence, "a malefic force that destroys through contagion anything that comes close to it" (Olson, 1994:237). Defilement, breaking the taboo, is the only way, according to Bataille, to approach or reside with the sacred. Conscious and ritualized transgression begin to function in a poststructuralist sense of breaking the binary of sacred/profane. By violating the interdiction, the ritualized transgression, particularly the sacrifice, dissolves these boundaries between God and creation and fills the gaps so that the former distinctions evaporate.

The sacrifice is not only an intentional transgression of the taboo on murder, but there is also the idea of the "sacrificial gift" which stands outside an economic system of fair exchange. The sacrificial gift, or offering is, for Bataille, "an unproductive expenditure that embodies the principle of absolute loss, i.e., loss without return" (Taylor, 1987:138). Bataille claims that the sacrifice, as prodigality, directly parallels the erotic:

> Erotic conduct is the opposite of normal conduct, as spending is the opposite of getting. If we follow the dictates of reason, we try to acquire all kinds of goods, we work in order to increase the sum of our possessions or of our knowledge, we use all means to get richer and to possess more. But when the fever of sex seizes us, we behave in the opposite way. We recklessly draw on our strength and sometimes in the violence of passion we squander considerable resources to no real purpose. Consequently, anything that suggests erotic excess always implies disorder. (Bataille, 1977:170)

The nature of the sacred is "prodigious effervescence of life," a pure excessiveness that emits energy spontaneously, freely expending, never with any expectation of reciprocity. Bataille argues that the world of labor and of exchange is merely a social one through which the human being smothers his or her true animal nature (which manifests itself in an acceptance of chaos and violence as natural occurrences) by creating rigid and arbitrary rules to create civilization. Every human, he argues, has an absolute propensity to break the bounds, to transgress in order "to expend and to exceed themselves and so communicate with the pure limitless being of the sacred" (Bataille, 1992:129, 61). Ritual sacrifice and sexual excess are the two most significant revealments of this urge to break away from the mundane toward the sacred (Bataille, 1962:94-116).

SACRIFICE, THE GIRARDIAN VICTIM AND THE LESBIAN MASOCHIST

Girard regards sacrifice as the act of making the offered victim or object sacred. He argues that the origin and continuity of all religion and of all culture resides interstitially between violence and desire, and that the source of all violence is desire. In order to oppose chaotic, destructive violence, Girard observes that the victim becomes the locus for "sanctioned" violence. Here, it is a violence played upon the body in order to avert or control destructive violence and to maintain social stability. In this way, the victim becomes god: he or she is not only endowed with the power to create danger, the victim, through violence, can end it as well. But the victim never knows, according to Girard, his or her part in the ritual, that is, until Jesus. I disagree with Girard on this point. Rather, the victim may or may not know its (or his or her) place in the ritual, the ritual is effective regardless. The victim becomes surrogate in order to perpetuate the original, socially and religiously formative event. Thus, the event takes place on three levels: "the surface level of observable behavior"; a "hidden" level of unconscious [or conscious] motivation; and the "generative" event, which Girard can imagine both as a "first time" and as a universal "moment" (Mack, 1987:10).

Both Girard and Bataille think that through the transformation of the crucifixion into the Eucharistic, bloodless sacrifice, Christianity has made sacrificial power impotent in modern Western context. Because of Christianity and its sanitization of the human sacrifice, Bataille asserts that the only accessible transgression left for the modern Western person is sexual excess. Girard does not really propose what the West uses in substitution for the lost sacrificial rites; he merely states that Westerners "seem to get along without them" (Williams, 1996:83). He suggests that since the sacrifice ritual can disappear from a society without devastating it is perhaps because there may be no real meaning behind the rites. He adds that it's no wonder ethnology and theology cannot determine the function of the ritual since the rites are dispensable. But why would a ritual so integral to the formation and maintenance of culture simply disappear and become obsolete? Rather, I wonder if Girard and the ethnologists and the theologians are looking in the right place. The sacrifice ritual exists but without "religious" signifiers. Again, Bataille makes this connection between religious ritual and sexual ritual, and particularly, between sacrifice and SM. He claims that the transgression itself is the intentional violence acted upon the thing being sacrificed. The only remnant of transgression available to the modern Western person, in Bataille's thinking, are those transgressions enacted in and sometimes particular to SM (1962, see the chapters on "De Sade and the Sovereign Man," "De Sade and the Normal Man," and "The Enigma of Incest"). However, even if a theorist, such as Bataille, recognizes the congruity between religious ritual and sexual ritual, the relationship between the two is usually an hierarchically dichotomous one of "good" and "bad," or "spiritual" and "physical." Religious ritual, specifically the sacrifice, is usually presumed to be the archetypal, original ritual while sexual ritual is a cheap imitation; it is a secondary occurrence in the event that religious ritual no longer functions.

For Bataille, the taboos of incest, gender role reversals and subversions of traditional power regimes hold the greatest potential for transgressive power. Lesbian SM incorporates, to a great extent, roles that play on those taboos Bataille deems particularly transgressive. For example, SM lesbians frequently act out the fantasies of daddy/daughter incest, rape, or master/slave in SM scenes. The power of the transgression becomes sharply defined against the backdrop of having a female lover who takes the role of a violent, male rapist; or two women playing out sex between a young daughter and a domineering, disciplinarian "dyke daddy" (see Califia, 1994 and also Scott, 1996:23-25).

In Jessica Benjamin's reading of Bataille and dominance/submission theory, she rightly observes that the Hegelian tension between recognition and difference and the Freudian split of ego is actually a tension that resides between life and death. But above all, she acknowledges the precise parallels that exist between sexual rituals in dominant/submissive relationships and rituals of sacrifice. For example, she writes that erotic masochism "expresses the same need for transcendence of self–the same flight from separation and discontinuity–formerly satisfied and expressed by religion" (Benjamin, 1983:296). She recognizes that in the parallel movement of both rituals, there are the same motives. One motive, according to Benjamin, is to maintain the tension between life and death or between the sacred and profane (1983:285). Another is to transcend rationality, or in other words, in SM, the masochist (female?) is rebelling against male rationality and control.

However, I am frustrated by two assumptions that are deeply embedded in Benjamin's work. She assumes without comment that religious ritual exists prior to sexual ritual. While Bataille and Girard claim the uselessness of sacrifice ritual in the modern Western world, Benjamin, and Bataille also, have observed that erotic ritual of domination-submission has stepped into that vacant spot and works toward the same ends, i.e., to sustain the tensions between life and death, between the sacred and profane. But for Benjamin, sexual ritual is clearly secondary and the similarities are probably mimetic of religious rite. Second, Benjamin continues to place all sexual ritual within Freud's Oedipal world. I am convinced, however, by the arguments given by psychoanalytic feminist critics of Freud which question whether all sexuality is locked within the Oedipal theory. Some assert that Lesbian SMists more that any other sexual group do not organize their sexuality around the father's phallus. Parveen Adams claims that there are three types of masochism: the religious flagellant, the "traditional" sex pervert, and the lesbian sadomasochist. She writes, "[Lesbian SMist] practices do indeed seem to be organized around disavowal and to be transgressive, but I will show that while they are indeed masochistic, nevertheless they constitute a new sexuality. The lesbian SMist takes full advantage of plasticity and movement: she constructs fetishes and substitutes them, tries them on like costumes" (Adams, 1989:262). Adams suggests that the lesbian SMist has rejected the phallus "without falling into a sickness" (1989:263). In the Freudian pathology of fetishism, the "pervert" disavows that the mother does not have a penis and endows another person or object with the phallus. That person or object becomes the point on which the "pervert" focuses his or her sexual desire, or rather, the fetish. Adams is suggesting here that the lesbian SMist, unlike Gay male to male SM or heterosexual SM, has somehow rejected the father's phallus altogether, without displacing it and without creating compulsion or pathology. Adams, perhaps following Irigaray, places the lesbian SMist outside the construct of a phallocentric culture.

In what follows, I propose that lesbian SM provides an arena for power play that utilizes both a Douglasian model of the body as symbol of a closed social system with Butler's notion of gender-role reversal as subversive. These theories parallel the violence to the body and the role-playing present in lesbian SM, which in turn conflate Bataille's two ultimate transgressions: sacrifice ritual and excessive sex.

THE INTERSECTION OF BODY AND CULTURE

Douglas comments that "the body is a model that can stand for any bounded system. Its boundaries can represent any boundaries which are threatened or precarious" (1966:115). If the body, in this instance, the lesbian body, stands for a closed social system, which is in this instance, the oppressive often violent system of patriarchy, then what that body does and what is done to and inscribed upon that body simulate what is being done by and to the signified social system. Butler, paraphrasing Douglas, notes that the limit of the body "is never merely material, but that the surface, the skin, is systemically signified by taboos and anticipated transgressions; indeed, the boundaries of the body become the limits of the social per se" (1990:131). The demarcation of the body may be perceived as becoming, according to Butler, "the limits of the socially hegemonic" (1990:131). The lesbian SM body playing (as parody, as simulation, as simulacra) the role of male oppressor inserts a kind of precategorical body into a social system (patriarchy) that views the body as a "medium that must be destroyed" (1990:130). At this point, i.e., the placement of the body into culture, the question becomes, What gets subverted? Does the body, if the skin is violated, its openings filled or emptied, indeed become subsumed into culture, or does the body retain a supposed original precategorical status? The point at which culture breaks the boundaries of the skin is the point that the social system and the body collide. The result is that the boundaries become blurred, the interiors of the body become exterior, they spill out into culture, and it is no longer clear where the body ends and culture begins: either culture subsumes the body or the body subverts culture. If the body is a lesbian SM body inserted into the role of patriarchal violator, and another lesbian SM body is cut open, actually or symbolically, the lesbian SM body cannot be subsumed by patriarchy (the principle critique of lesbian SM by radical feminists) because lesbian SM both mimics the role of violator and freely, prodigally opens the body to culture.

Non-lesbian SM bodies, i.e., heterosexual SMists and Gay male SMists, risk being enveloped by patriarchy because the initial boundaries are not concretized, i.e., there is no clear distinction between the players and the reality; the subversive power contained in gender and sex role-reversals is absent. The man as actor or as submissive cannot reject and simulate, rather, the scene does become replication. If men are involved in perpetuating the roles they are already given in patriarchy, nothing is really being subverted. The profundity of the transgression dissipates if a man is involved, as the "rapist" or the "daddy" or as a slave, because the subversion occurs at the level of the rejection of the phallus, which the SM lesbian rejects as symbolic of oppression and violence against women. The lesbian SMist then reclaims the phallus and subverts the hegemonic power, the phallus and the violence for her own sexual pleasure. Since lesbians have already rejected the subjectivity of the penis, lesbian SM can then reappropriate the provinces of power it resists. Even as a bottom or as the "little boy" of a dominant female, the male masochist cannot exist outside phallocentric culture nor can he actually break away from the pathology that forms his masochism (Adams, 1989:261). Conversely, as Butler writes, "Lesbian sexuality can be understood to redeploy its 'derivativeness' in the service of displacing hegemonic heterosexual norms" (1991:17). The lesbian subjectivity that occurs as a result of being outside a phallocentric culture is precisely why role reversal is particularly powerful for SM lesbians.

Therefore, as I have illustrated above, the subversiveness and transgressiveness of lesbian SM is not only the radical role-playing/role-reversal of patriarchal and hegemonic oppression, but it is also the actual presence of physical violence, pain and suffering in lesbian SM as well. The simulation of oppressive, patriarchal gender roles (following Butler) from beyond phallocentric culture, coexisting with the cutting of the body and other violations to the body (following Douglas) parallel the two primary transgressions according to Bataille: excessive sex and sacrifice. Recalling Bataille, the point of dynamic tension, culture on the brink of chaos and the flows of the opened body, are of the sacred. I suggest that certain rituals played out in scenes by SM lesbians resuscitate the symbol of ritual sacrifice so that it is again transgressive thus powerful within the modern Western context. Bataille's observation that, "Nowadays sacrifice is outside the field of our experience and imagination must do duty for the real thing," is no longer true (1962:91). The lesbian masochist is the Girardian surrogate victim. Her body is the site of controlled violence so that the destructive violence all around her is held at bay. Many lesbian women have recognized the socio/political power in the theater of SM. Whether or not the participants recognize the subversive potential of SM, it exists nonetheless. There may be violence inflicted on flesh, there may be blood, there may be degradation and humiliation, because SM rituals must be dangerous, dark and violent rituals to be transformative.

Finally, one conclusion I can draw from this ever-complex issue of women's sexuality is that there is much more going on here than the embodiment and erotification of patriarchal violence, which, as I have pointed out, is the dominant accusation by many feminists. Since SM functions on so many levels in the lives of lesbian women, a feminist hermeneutic of women's sexuality should recognize the lived value of those practices. This hermeneutic should take care not to assume the constructed hierarchies of sexual value, thus totalizing the SM lesbian as inferior other.

There is a shared position of all women being that they exist and thrive (or not) in a patriarchal society. In lesbian SM, the violences of patriarchy are worked through, acted out, in a safe, consensual space where the patriarchal power games at least have the potential of being elided or to be acted out in such a way as to nullify their power. Lesbian sadomasochism is not, as Bataille would say, a part of that faction which maintains structure and order; it is, like feminism, "a revolt, a refusal of the proposed condition" (Boldt-Irons, 1995:234).

REFERENCES

Adams, Parveen. 1989. "Of Female Bondage." *Between Feminism and Psychoanalysis*, ed. Teresa Brennan. New York: Routledge, 247-65.

Bataille, Georges. 1962. *Eroticism*. London: Marion Boyars Publishers.

_____ . 1977. *Death and Sensuality: A Study of Eroticism and the Taboo*. New York: Arno Press.

_____ . 1989. *Theory of Religion*. New York: Zone Books.

_____ . 1992. *The Accursed Share*, v. II. New York: Zone Books.

Benjamin, Jessica. 1983. "Master and Slave: The Fantasy of Erotic Domination." Snitow, Stansell and Thompson, eds. *Powers of Desire*. New York: Monthly Review Press, 280-299.

_____ . 1988. *The Bonds of Love: Psychoanalysis, Feminism and the Problem of Domination*. New York: Pantheon.

Boldt-Irons, Leslie A. ed. 1995. *On Bataille: Critical Essays.* Albany: State University of New York Press.

Butler, Judith. 1990. *Gender Trouble.* New York: Routledge.

_____ . 1991. "Imitation and Gender Subordination." Diana Fuss, ed. *Inside/ Out: Lesbian Theories, Gay Theories.* New York: Routledge, 13-31.

Califia, Pat. 1994. *Doing it for Daddy.* Boston: Alyson Publications, Inc.

Douglas, Mary. 1966. *Purity and Danger: An Analysis of Concepts of Pollution and Taboo.* London: Routledge.

Dworkin, Andrea. 1981. *Pornography: Men Possessing Women.* New York: Perigree.

_____ . 1987. *Intercourse.* New York: Free Press.

Girard, Rene. 1978. *Violence and the Sacred.* Baltimore: Johns Hopkins University.

Hopkins, Patrick D. 1994. "Rethinking Sadomasochism: Feminism, Interpretation, and Simulation." *Hypatia* 9.1:116-141.

Mack, Burton. 1987. "Introduction: Religion and Ritual." *Violent Origins: Ritual Killing and Cultural Formation*, Robert G. Hamerton-Kelly, ed. Stanford: Stanford University Press.

Olson, Carl. 1994. "Eroticism, Violence, and Sacrifice: A Postmodern Theory of Religion and Ritual." *Theory in the Study of Religion* 6.3: 231-250.

Scott, D. Travers. 1996. "Jaymie." *Pucker Up* 1.2:23-25.

Taylor, Mark C. 1987. *Altarity.* Chicago: Chicago University Press.

Tong, Rosemary. 1989. *Feminist Thought: A Comprehensive Introduction.* San Francisco: West View Press.

Truscott, Carol. 1991. "SM: Some Questions and a Few Answers." *Leatherfolk: Radical Sex, People, Politics, and Practice*, Mark Thompson, ed. Boston: Alyson Publications, Inc., 15-36.

Turner, Victor. 1969. *The Ritual Process: Structure and Anti-Structure.* Chicago: Aldine.

Williams, James G. ed. 1996. *The Girard Reader.* New York: Crossroad Press.

The Materiality of Gender:
Looking for Lesbian Bodies
in Transgender History

Nan Alamilla Boyd

SUMMARY. Lesbian and transgender histories often recuperate the same historical figures; however, many lesbian spaces (like the Michigan Womyn's Music Festival) have excluded lesbian-identified male-to-female transsexuals. Through an analysis of historical inclusion and socio-political exclusion, this essay examines the relationship between "birth bodies," gender and sexuality. It argues that the lesbian body appears in history through the naturalization of "birth-bodies" and the recuperation of cross-gender behavior. In this

Nan Alamilla Boyd has a PhD from Brown University. She currently teaches queer studies, Latina studies, and U.S. women's history in the Women's Studies Program at the University of Colorado at Boulder where she also chairs the Program in Lesbian, Gay, Bisexual and Transgender Studies. Her book, *Wide Open Town: San Francisco's Lesbian and Gay History*, is forthcoming by University of California Press.

Address correspondence to: Nan Alamilla Boyd, Women's Studies, University of Colorado, Boulder, CO 80309-0246 (E-mail: alamilla@spot.colorado.edu).

The author thanks CLAGS, the Center for Lesbian and Gay Studies, for funding that supported this research.

This paper was delivered at the Organization of American Historians Annual Meetings, Chicago, Illinois, March 28-31, 1996.

Another version of this article was published in *A Queer World: The Center for Lesbian and Gay Studies Reader*, ed. Martin Duberman (New York: New York University Press, 1997).

[Haworth co-indexing entry note]: "The Materiality of Gender: Looking for Lesbian Bodies in Transgender History." Boyd, Nan Alamilla. Co-published simultaneously in *Journal of Lesbian Studies* (The Haworth Press, Inc.) Vol. 3, No. 3, 1999, pp. 73-81; and: *Lesbian Sex Scandals: Sexual Practices, Identities, and Politics* (ed: Dawn Atkins) The Haworth Press, Inc., 1999, pp. 73-81; and: *Lesbian Sex Scandals: Sexual Practices, Identities, and Politics* (ed: Dawn Atkins) Harrington Park Press, an imprint of The Haworth Press, Inc., 1999, pp. 73-81. Single or multiple copies of this article are available for a fee from The Haworth Document Delivery Service [1-800-342-9678, 9:00 a.m. - 5:00 p.m. (EST). E-mail address: getinfo@haworthpressinc.com].

73

way, the body becomes a template for lesbian historical recuperation and an organizing principle for contemporary lesbian communities. *[Article copies available for a fee from The Haworth Document Delivery Service: 1-800-342-9678. E-mail address: getinfo@haworthpressinc.com]*

On the day before Thanksgiving in 1947, FBI agents visited David Warren at his remote Sonoma County farm to question him about his draft record. Instead they arrested both Warren and his wife, Thelma Jane Walter, on felony counts for perjury, conspiracy, and impersonation in marriage. Warren was, in fact, a woman, the newspaper coverage explains, and the two had wed six months prior at a local church because they "considered living together without being married very improper." Early the next year, another "male impersonator," Charles H. Largey, who worked as an elevator operator in San Francisco's financial district, was arrested for passing bad checks. Upon arrest, a journalist noted, he changed from his elevator uniform "to a man's sport costume." Unlike many "impersonators" who explain their crossdressing as an economic necessity and, hoping for leniency, appear in court in "appropriate" clothing, both Warren and Largey appeared before the judge in men's clothing. "I always wanted to be a man," Largey explained. "When I'm not [forced to dress as a woman] I always go as one." Warren, who had attended the University of California, also did not try to hide his gender identity. Describing himself as a "frustrated girl who always wanted to be a boy," he explained that "doctors told us that some day surgeons might work such a transformation."[1]

These examples frame a tension in lesbian and transgender historiography.[2] Were David Warren and Thelma Jane Walter lesbians who hid their outlaw sexuality behind a heterosexual facade? Or were David Warren and Charles Largey men who articulated a transgender identity at a time when language failed to describe their experiences? Both lesbian and transgender communities look to the past to recuperate individuals who proudly or cleverly lived outlaw sexualities or genders. However, because of the slippage between sexuality and gender, lesbian and transgender communities often spin usable histories around the same figures. In lesbian historiography, for example, "butch" drag (or female-to-male cross-dressing) signals the presence of lesbians. In a U.S. working-class context, butch iconography is lesbian iconography, and masculine gender codes when worn on an anatomically female body advertise lesbian desire and sexuality (Nestle, 1987, 1992; Kennedy and Davis, 1993). Because of the relationship between butchness and lesbian sexuality, lesbian histories often conflate butch cross-dressing (anatomical females sporting masculine appearance for the purpose of advertising lesbian sexuality) with female-to-male passing (anatomical females donning masculine appearance for the purpose of being perceived by others as men). Lesbian history, particularly in its earlier phase, documented the history of passing women because these individuals (when "discovered" to be women) were the most visible and publicly accessible historical subjects (Katz, 1976:209-279).[3] Transgender histories take a different approach to the historical recuperation of male-appearing individuals who are "discovered" through death or arrest to be anatomically female. They argue that many "male impersonators," because of their life circumstances and daily practice, are more accurately understood as transgendered men rather than passing women or cross-dressing lesbians (Cromwell, 1994; Stryker, 1995; Jones, 1994).

The slide show *She Even Chewed Tobacco* discusses cross-dressing and passing women in U.S. Western history. Created in 1979, it introduces the character Babe Bean, a "passing woman" who lived in Stockton, California from 1897-1898. It places Bean within a narrative about women's history that suggests that passing women functioned as a cultural precursor to contemporary butch lesbians (San Francisco Lesbian and Gay History Project 1979, 1989). The slide show's introductory segment states that in the nineteenth century, "a small but significant group of American women rejected the limitations of the female sphere and claimed the privileges enjoyed by men. They worked for men's wages, courted and married the women they loved and even voted. They did so by adopting men's clothing, hiding their female identities from most of the world and passing as men." *She Even Chewed Tobacco* uses passing women as liminal characters to highlight the gulf between male privilege and female oppression. It positions them within a late-1970s feminist discourse that stresses labor equity, suffrage rights, and lesbian love. Moreover, it tells a Horatio Alger-esque story, embedding a nationalist trope of success within feminist discourse: successful cross-dressing produced women who could vote. In this way, *She Even Chewed Tobacco* gives nineteenth-century female-to-male cross-dressers a history as women within the rubric of contemporary lesbian and feminist concerns. No mention is made of transgender identity, and the only conclusion one might make about the lives of passing women is that if they lived at a time when they could enjoy economic freedom, political rights, or sexual love for women *as women*, they would not choose to masquerade as men. Indeed, it is the concept of masquerade that underscores the argument that nineteenth- and twentieth-century female-to-male cross-dressers were really women and, in fact, probably lesbians.

Babe Bean is a complicated historical figure, however, because for a short period of time Bean straddled the boundary between man and woman. In August 1897, Bean was arrested in Stockton, California for crossdressing. After the arrest s/he stayed in Stockton for approximately a year and became something of a local celebrity. Bean continued to dress entirely in men's clothing, lived alone on a houseboat, and attended meetings at the local Bachelor's Club. However, Bean communicated only through writing and refused to speak aloud, shrouding the "truth" of her/his sex. In other words, even though Bean admitted to having a female body, her/his self-presentation was so consistently masculine that some of the citizens of Stockton remained unconvinced of Bean's sex. "The mystery is still unsolved as to whether 'Babe' Bean is a boy or girl, a man or a woman," one news article reported, dubbing Bean "the mysterious girl-boy, man-woman" (Sullivan, 1990:31).

In 1898, Bean left Stockton for San Francisco and joined the U.S. military, serving as a journalist in the Philippines during the Spanish-American War. Bean returned to San Francisco after the war, his arms covered with elaborate tattoos, and he adopted the name Jack Garland. At this time in San Francisco, 1903, cross-dressing was made illegal by city ordinance. Garland spent the rest of his life in San Francisco, working as a male nurse and a free-lance social worker, and he was not arrested again. However, when Jack Garland died in 1936, after almost forty years of living as a man, his "true sex" was revealed to be female. Jack Garland was born in 1869, daughter of José Marcos Mugarrieta, San Francisco's first Mexican consul, and Eliza Alice Garland (Hyman, 1936).

Lou Sullivan, a female-to-male (FTM) transsexual and also an active member of San Francisco's Gay and Lesbian Historical Society, published a biography of Jack Garland in 1990 entitled *From Female to Male, The Life of Jack Bee Garland* which retextualizes Babe Bean's life as a passing woman and recuperates it as the life of Jack Garland, a man. Sullivan states in his introduction that "Jack Garland demonstrated, through his lifelong adherence to his male identity, that his reasons for living as a man were more complex than just his dissatisfaction with the way society expected women to dress. [Jack Garland] was a female-to-male transsexual" (Sullivan, 1990:3). Furthermore, while many histories of female-to-male crossdressers tell the story of how passing women were able to pursue the women they loved under the protective cover of male dress and, perhaps, male identity, this was not the case for Jack Garland. Garland preferred the company of men. Sullivan notes that "he dressed and lived as a man in order to be a man among men"—a gay man, perhaps—which further unhinges any direct connection between cross-gender behavior and sexuality. In the memoirs he left behind, Jack Garland states that "Many have thought it strange that I do not care to mingle with women of my own age, and seem partial to men's company. Well, is it not natural that I should prefer the companionship of men? I am never happy nor contented unless with a few of 'the boys'" (Sullivan, 1990:4).

While Sullivan rewrites lesbian history to produce a history of visible transsexuals, one cannot overlook Garland's racial, ethnic, class, and national passings. The turn of the century was a period of intense racial and national consolidation which marked the rise of Anglo-Saxonism, the production of a nationalist discourse of U.S. exceptionalism, and intensified U.S. colonization. Garland's gender certainly did not exist independent of these circumstances. Garland chose Anglo names for himself signaling a movement toward white-ethnic or Anglo-American identifications. Moreover, while his silence in Stockton masked, most obviously, the feminine tenor of his voice, it also hid Spanish language inflections that would have destabililzed his Anglo identification. Also, for the last decades of his life, Garland wandered the streets of San Francisco and lived in poverty. Here, gender remains inseparable from class; while Garland's maleness allowed for late-night street wandering and urban rescue work, the very public and class-specific (impoverished) nature of his activities reinforced his gender. Finally, Garland's participation in the Spanish-American War and his service to the U.S. military wrapped a cloak of nationalist allegiance around his political subjectivity, enhancing his masculinity through patriotism.

Babe Bean/Jack Garland's multiple passings complicate his historical recuperation as either lesbian or transsexual. Moreover, his multiple historical recuperations highlight a conundrum in contemporary queer historiography. Namely: who are the subjects of lesbian and transgender history? What is the meaning of cross-gender behavior and identity? What is the material substance that determines the truth of one's gendered or sexual identity? Is it self-articulation, sexual activity, daily practice, popular perception, or genital status? In lesbian history, genital status often reveals the "truth" about sex and gender. In other words, we "know" Babe Bean's "true sex" because she had a vagina, and as a result, we "know" her gender. If Bean had had sexual relations with another person with a vagina, then we "know" they were lesbians. The category lesbian slips seamlessly from biological sex to gender and sexuality. While the historical recuperation of "passing women" (like David Warren or Charles Largey) creates a broad and usable past for lesbians, it conflates sex, gender, and sexuality, naturalizing birth bodies as a primary source of information about lesbian sexuality. Biological sex thus becomes the fountain of truth, the foundation of knowledge about lesbian history.

Controversies surrounding the Michigan Womyn's Music Festival's entrance policies frame these questions from a different angle. This festival, which has been in existence for twenty years, is a week-long event where thousands of women gather in a Michigan forest to camp, socialize, attend workshops, and enjoy an impressive line-up of mostly lesbian musicians. Until 1991, the festival had no explicit policy with regard to the attendance of transsexuals (or defining exactly who "womyn" are), but in 1991 Nancy Jean Burkholder was expelled from the festival after one day of attendance because she was suspected of being a transsexual. Burkholder was not the first transsexual woman to enter the festival; in fact, she had attended the year before. In August 1991, Burkholder was expelled because (even though this policy remained absent from festival literature) a "security guard" asserted that "transsexuals were not permitted to attend the festival." Before she left, however, the security guard asked Burkholder whether she had had a sex change operation. Burkholder told the guard she could look at her genitals, but Burkholder maintained that her surgical history was her own business (Burkholder, 1993). This information signals an ambiguity in the festival's policy. Burkholder was being ejected, but was it because of her surgical history, her genital status, her consciousness, or her chromosomes? The security guard stated that the festival had a "no transsexuals" policy, and while this may be true, her curiosity about Burkholder's surgical history suggests that birth bodies had, indeed, more to do with one's relationship to the category "womyn" than identity, consciousness, or current genital status.

As a result of these events, the 1992 Michigan Womyn's Music Festival's literature became more explicit of its policies, stating that the festival was open to "womyn-born-womyn" only. No transsexuals were expelled from the 1992 festival (even though there were several in attendance), but the next year's festival saw the expulsion of four male-to-female (MTF) transsexual lesbians and the birth of "Camp Trans," a quasi-refugee colony that pitched tent just outside the entrance to the festival. From this venue transsexuals and friends continued to distribute literature about the festival's exclusionary policy in an attempt to gauge whether the producers' policies matched those of the festival-goers. Through the next year, the spring and summer of 1994, the protesters pressured the festival producers, Lisa Vogel and Barbara Price, to state explicitly that their "womyn-born-womyn only" policy really meant that the festival was open to non-transsexual women only, which would raise the stakes not only to the level of explicit discrimination but closer to the body where one might measure one's transsexual-ness against surgical or hormonal intervention. However, the festival producers refused to change their "womyn-born-womyn" policy and in August 1994 "Camp Trans, for humyn born humyns" re-seated itself, hosting a wealth of extracurricular activities, again just outside the entrance of the festival.

On the sixth day of the 1994 festival, after a group of protesters walked to the front gate and challenged the festival's entrance policy with a variety of differently sexed and gendered bodies, and Lesbian Avengers gathered momentum inside the festival in defense of excluded (transsexual) Lesbian Avengers on the outside, the producers agreed to allow transsexuals to enter the festival–but still under the rubric of "womyn-born-womyn" (Gabriel, 1995; Wilchins, 1995). This constituted a victory for the protesters in that the meaning of gender was placed within the realm of self-definition, but questions of morphology continued to plague the policing of borders. It remained unclear whether non- or pre-operative MTF transsexuals might enter the festival or whether FTMs at any stage remained within the rubric of "womyn-born-womyn." In other words, how much or in what ways did the body constitute consciousness? Could consciousness exist irrelevant to the body's contours? Could individuals with penises be "womyn-born-womyn"? Might individuals with vaginas be men (Rubin, 1996; Singer, 1996; Hale, 1996)?

The Michigan Womyn's Music Festival's struggle to protect a politicized and gender-specific territory mirrors the recuperation of lesbians in history in that when push comes to shove, real lesbians are measured against a template of "natural-born" bodies. At the Michigan Womyn's Music Festival, male-to-female transsexuals are not "womyn" because even if their surgical history remains invisible to the naked eye, their "natural" sex and gender remains male. In lesbian history, female-to-male crossdressers, particularly those with female-gendered lovers, are often recuperated as lesbians even if their gender remains consistently male: their "natural" sex (and thus sexuality) remains female. In both examples, naturalized articulations of the body draw functional boundaries around the lesbian community. Birth bodies, coded in binary opposition, hegemonically police lesbian space and lesbian territory.

In conclusion, the lesbian body materializes in history–and lesbian histories materialize–through the reiteration of gender ideologies that ground sex and sexuality in naturalized understandings of how bodies function: sexually, socially, and politically. These examples illustrate the assumptions that bodies born with penises are not able to express female gender or lesbian sexuality and do not belong in lesbian space. Bodies born with vaginas, despite male gender identification, remain lesbian. In this way, the body becomes a marker for comprehending and translating lesbian historical narrative; it becomes the material of historical memory.

The recuperation of lesbian history is a vital, rich, and fascinating project, which, even in its undervalued and underfunded infancy, functions as powerful structuring paradigm. Lesbian historiography naturalizes the body when the materiality of gender and sexuality defaults back to an examination of genitals. As a result, morphology remains central to the construction of contemporary lesbian identity, both in and through history.

NOTES

1. "Girl, 'Husband, Wife' in Court," *Santa Rosa Press Democrat* (11/29/47); "Two Girls Who 'Wed' Must Face Court Today," *Santa Rosa Press Democrat* (11/28/47); "Police Unmask Woman Faker," *San Francisco Examiner*, 4/1/48. Transgender Clippings File, San Francisco Gay and Lesbian Historical Society.

2. This essay uses the term "transgender" as a general category that contains within it more specific social identities such as transsexual, transvestite, cross-dresser, butch, and queen. However, it is often very important to distinguish between the terms "transsexual" and "transgender" since access to medical technologies and state entitlements (i.e., change of name, alteration of birth certificate) are dependent on a psychiatric diagnosis of "transsexualism." In other words, the term "transsexual" signifies (at times) a formal and technical relationship with doctors and the state with regard to "sex reassignment" while the term transgender does not. For diagnostic categories, see the American Psychiatric Association's *Diagnostic and Statistical Manual of Mental Disorders*, 4th ed. (1994). For a more comprehensive discussion of the term "transgender" and its relationship to transsexuality, see Susan Stryker (1994), and for more information about FTM surgeries, see James Green (1995).

3. Esther Neston (1984) problematizes the slippage between masculinity and lesbianism, and Joan Nestle, Elizabeth Kennedy and Madeline Davis clarify the distinction between passing women and butch lesbians by articulating in rich detail the function of butch gender as a component of lesbian desire and representation (Nestle, 1987, 1992; Kennedy and Davis, 1993).

REFERENCES

Burkholder, Nancy Jean. 1993. "A Kinder, Gentler Festival?" *TransSisters* 2 (November/December): 4.

Cromwell, Jason. 1994. "Default Assumptions, or The Billy Tipton Phenomenon," *FTM* 28: 4-5.

Gabriel, Davina Anne. 1995. "Mission to Michigan III: Barbarians at the Gates," *TransSisters* 7: 14-23.

Green, James. 1995. "Getting Real about FTM Surgery," *Chrysalis: The Journal of Transgressive Gender Identities* 2(2): 27-32.

Hale, C. Jacob. 1996. "Dyke Leatherboys and Their Daddies: How to Have Sex without Men or Women." Paper delivered at the Berkshire Conference on the History of Women.

Hyman, A.D. 1936. "Death Reveals S.F. Writer's Pose as Man," *San Francisco Chronicle* (9/21/36): 1, 4.

Jones, Jordy. 1994. "FTM Crossdresser Murdered," *FTM* 26: 3.

Katz, Jonathan. 1976. "Passing Women" In *Gay American History.* New York: Thomas Crowell Co., 209-279.

Kennedy, Elizabeth Lapovsky and Madeline D. Davis. 1993. *Boots of Leather, Slippers of Gold: The History of a Lesbian Community.* New York: Routledge.

Nestle, Joan. 1987. *A Restricted Country.* Ithaca, New York: Firebrand.

Nestle, Joan, ed. 1992. *The Persistent Desire: A Femme-Butch Reader.* Boston: Alyson.

Neston, Esther. 1984. "The Mythic Mannish Lesbian: Radclyffe Hall and the New Woman," *Signs* 9(4): 557-75.

Rubin, Henry Samuel. 1996. "Transformations: Emerging Female to Male Transsexual Identities." Ph.D. dissertation, Brandeis University.

San Francisco Lesbian and Gay History Project. 1979; rpt 1990. *She Even Chewed Tobacco.* 32 min. Distributed by Women Make Movies. Videocassette.

San Francisco Lesbian and Gay History Project. 1989. "'She Even Chewed Tobacco': A Pictorial Narrative of Passing Women in America." In Martin Duberman, Martha Vicinus, George Chauncey Jr., eds. *Hidden from History: Reclaiming the Gay and Lesbian Past,* 183-194. New York: Penguin.

Singer, Ben. 1996. "Velveteen Realness." Paper delivered at the CLAGS Trans/Forming Knowledge Conference.

Stryker, Susan. 1994. "My Words to Victor Frankenstein above the Village of Chamounix," *GLQ: Gay Lesbian Quarterly* 1(3):251-52.

Stryker, Susan. 1995. "Local Transsexual history," *TNT: Transsexual News Telegraph* 5 (Summer-Autumn 1995) 14-15.

Sullivan, Louis. 1990. *From Female to Male: The Life of Jack Bee Garland.* Boston, Alyson Press.

Wilchins, Riki Anne. 1995. "The Menace in Michigan," *Gendertrash* 3: 17-19.

Toward a Dyke Discourse:
The Essentially Constructed
Stonebutch Identity

Robin Maltz

SUMMARY. This essay argues the need for a dyke discourse that is a parallel project to queer theory but considers female subjectivity first and foremost and pays specific attention to desire and sexual practice as a mode of identity formation. The primary subject is the stonebutch–a queer masculine female, not a woman/not a man–and her partnered identity, the straight-appearing femme. Together, they fall out of the "woman-loving-woman" definition of lesbian, and problematize feminism's evacuation of female gender difference and assimiliationist strategies. *[Article copies available for a fee from The Haworth Document Delivery Service: 1-800-342-9678. E-mail address: getinfo@haworthpressinc.com]*

UNDOING DADDY

"Daddy" gets ready to go out for the evening. She showers, uses men's cologne, combs hair wax into her buzzcut to keep it upright. Tattoos

Robin Maltz is a femmedyke scholar and mother who is currently a PhD candidate in the Department of Performance Studies at New York University. Her work is primarily in queer female femininity and masculinity.

Address correspondence to: Robin Maltz, 17 New Jersey Avenue, Bellport, NY 11713 (E-mail: ram3616@is2.nyu.edu).

[Haworth co-indexing entry note]: "Toward a Dyke Discourse: The Essentially Constructed Stonebutch Identity." Maltz, Robin. Co-published simultaneously in *Journal of Lesbian Studies* (The Haworth Press, Inc.) Vol. 3, No. 3, 1999, pp. 83-92; and: *Lesbian Sex Scandals: Sexual Practices, Identities, and Politics* (ed: Dawn Atkins) The Haworth Press, Inc., 1999, pp. 83-92; and: *Lesbian Sex Scandals: Sexual Practices, Identities, and Politics* (ed: Dawn Atkins) Harrington Park Press, an imprint of The Haworth Press, Inc., 1999, pp. 83-92. Single or multiple copies of this article are available for a fee from The Haworth Document Delivery Service [1-800-342-9678, 9:00 a.m. - 5:00 p.m. (EST). E-mail address: getinfo@haworthpressinc.com].

encircle her arms, chest and back; queering her female body. She slips her legs into a leather harness, slides her butch cock through the hole in the center, and snaps it tightly around her hips. She pulls on her jockstrap, and adjusts the cock so that the balls are pressed against her genitals. She's wearing a softer cock, the one she packs but does not fuck with. The packing dick is in repose and Daddy likes the weight of it in her Levi's. The dick she uses on her femme is six thick inches. Both cocks are hyper-representational in appearance, with prominent heads, shafts, veins and testicles.

A binder, similar to an ace bandage, holds Daddy's ample breasts to her chest beneath a dark men's-tailored shirt; leather suspenders curve ever so slightly over her chest. A stonefemme reads "binding" and "packing" as the signifiers of a stonebutch, but Daddy will tell you that she packs and binds when she is alone. Heightened masculinity foregrounded on a subverted female body is erotic, autoerotic, and personally validating for a stonebutch.

Daddy's babydoll is "girl." (My use of the lower-case "g" throughout this essay is intentional as a literary device to imply subordination.) girl is not a pouting child in a party dress. She is a stonefemme who will not be melted by any ordinary lesbian or soft butch who expects sexual reciprocity. If her lover is submissive sexually, girl is not interested. She also does not want to be left carrying the groceries in her high heels or open her own doors, thank you very much.

girl admires the bulge in Daddy's pants, his dominance, his gentlemanliness, his uncompromising masculinity, the way he takes up space with his authority. A stonebutch's tough demeanor is an advertisement, a promise of sexual mastery. Daddy has his way with girl. He is her top. Daddy orchestrates the sex acts—with virility, dominance, and prowess. girl is the recipient, she is the bottom, the butch's submissive other. Daddy touches her when he wants to, pulls that girl onto his lap, onto his butchcock, strokes girl's meaty thighs. He is dominance to her submission. Dominance and submission as a lifestyle, not an s/m negotiation. They have an unspoken erotic arrangement between them; a consensual agreement to be unequals.

Daddy and girl are members of a proliferating stone butch/femme community that has formed in recent years through Internet access and now meets in real life in various U.S. cities. The Internet lists with names such as "stonebutch," and stone butch/femme Internet Relay Chats (IRC) are a cyber "bar" culture of sorts. The stone butch/femme members of the contemporary virtual community coalesce from a broad range of geographical, class, cultural, economic, racial, and ethnic backgrounds. They frequently arrive on the lists with very similar notions about their identity and desires, but many, if not most, did not have the language to define themselves. The boundaries, rules, and concepts that constitute contemporary stone identity are continually being negotiated and reworked on the Internet lists, especially since the proliferation of other forms of female masculinity and gender expression in recent years–namely, female-to-male (FtM) transgender identity and the availability of sexual reassignment surgery for transsexuals. Yet some standards are set in stone, so to speak, and these "laws of stoneness" quickly distinguish the stones from the soft butches, femme tops, lesbians, and other modes of dykeness that do not have an integral need for the binary of dyke femininity/masculinity.

What makes a stonebutch "stone" is a source of frequent contestation. At one time, "untouchability" was the foremost determiner of stoneness in a butch. According to historians Elizabeth Kennedy and Madeline Davis (1993), "a stone butch does all the doin' and does not allow her lover to reciprocate in kind. To be untouchable meant to gain pleasure solely from giving pleasure" (1993:192). To be untouchable was also a test of a butch's masculinity. To "flip" a butch, or "melt" a butch meant that the butch was vulnerable and vulnerability was not perceived as a masculine trait (1993:209).

In the contemporary stonebutch/femme community, stoneness has become less about untouchability and more about a butch's relationship to masculinity–although many of the other 1940s and '50s standards continue to be honored such as masculine butch and feminine femme clothing styles and aesthetics, gendered domestic arrangements, and a certain butch chivalry and femme delicacy. This does not mean that what a butch and femme do in bed is not relevant to stone identity. In the last couple decades, in a climate celebrating diverse sexuality, stone couples have opened up to one another about what it means for a stonebutch to achieve sexual pleasure. Most stonebutches achieve heightened sexual pleasure through acts of imagination that are physically enacted and reified by their femme lovers.

Take Daddy's dick for instance. It is not a "dildo" nor a "sex toy." Its presence resignifies her body for both herself and her lovers. As Daddy describes it,

> girl speaks my language. She knows she can't approach me like I was a woman, which is the mistake others have made. She never tries to feminize me. She's got no stake in it. She mediates through my dick and so I trust her with my dream. Our dream. Our extremist dream of my masculinity taking her femininity played out in these two female bodies.

girl's sexual expertise, her erotic power as a stonefemme is her ability to invest her butch's masculinity with meaning. She gives life to that butchcock between his legs whether it's strapped on or in a drawer, because essentially, it is always there. She knows how to touch her Daddy's female body sensually and erotically within the boundaries established by her butch's needs. Stonebutch tits are resignified as pecs and molded silicon becomes genitals, feeling more real than her biological ones. girl invests Daddy's resignified body with realness out of her own desire and need. It is a relationship of the imagination bound by trust. Daddy says,

> I was untouchable–or tolerated being touched now and then though I didn't like it. Female sexuality, a cunt, was what my lover had, not me. She was the woman, I was the stonebutch. I was with plenty of women who didn't understand what that meant. They wanted me to do them and then roll over and get done, the way lesbians do.

girl says,

> I am a femme who loves stones because what I want to do is show my appreciation and love for the masculinity that makes a stone-butch who he is. I don't want to be with feminine women, lesbians, or men. I do not want to be with a butch bottom because I don't want to be sexually dominant. I make my butch's body feel masculine because I need it to be that way and so does he. We never talk about his breasts or vagina. In bed I admire his strong tattooed chest and hard cock.

A STONE LINEAGE

Stone butch/femme lifestyle and desire of the 1940s-60s is well documented in historical accounts such as Kennedy and Davis's *Boots of Leather, Slippers of Gold* (1993), fiction based on autobiography such as *Stone Butch Blues* (1993) by Leslie Feinberg, and pulp fiction heroes like Ann Bannon's butch protagonist *Beebo Brinker* (1962). There is no clear consensus as to when the term "stonebutch" came into use; it may have originated in 1940s and '50s Black butch/femme communities. It is also unclear whether stone meant "utterly, entirely" as in stone-cold, stone-broke. In any case, stonebutch identity predates its naming. Stephen Gordon, the protagonist of Radclyffe Hall's *The Well of Loneliness* (1928) was a stonebutch. Freud's unidentified patient in "The Psychogenesis of a

Case of Homosexuality in a Woman" (1920), who clearly baffled him with her masculine yearnings and behavior, was a stonebutch.

These narratives of stonebutch subjectivity (prior to its naming), are linked by the relationship of the subject to queer masculinity–both in gender expression and sexual orientation. The more masculine the female the more enigmatic she was to those who wanted to understand her desire and gender. There is no question, in the above narratives and others that describe female masculinity prior to lesbian feminism, that masculinity on a female "invert" was not a performance or role-playing. Although deemed pathological, it was considered essential, integral to her being.

In the early narratives, the masculine female invert was considered to be a single subjectivity, a homosexual without a homosexual object of desire. Her object of desire was assumed to be a heterosexual woman tricked by the wiles of the masculine female or falling prey to a female passing as a male. The femme, prior to her naming, was given no agency of her own and was assumed to be a bored heterosexual woman looking for a thrill. It wasn't until around the 1930s in the United States that femme subjectivity became the partnered identity of the butch. Partnering the butch with another female homosexual brought the dyad of butch/femme into language as a female homosexual couple. To quote Sue-Ellen Case (1988), "the butch-femme couple inhabit the subject position together . . . they are not split subjects" (in 1993:295). Just as Bonnie enhanced Clyde's outlawness, the coupling of the butch with the femme as a single subjectivity provided a new threat to the norms of patriarchy, which I will elaborate on momentarily.

The onus of shame, freakishness, and gender dysphoria followed the stonebutch from the sexologists of the late 19th century through 1970s lesbian feminism to the present. In 1956 the Daughters of Bilitis (founded by Phyllis Lyon and Del Martin in 1955), published an influential newsletter called *The Ladder*. The doctrine of the DOB, as specified in *The Ladder*, was that lesbians should rise above the bar culture and in particular they should dress in an appropriate feminine manner (Burana et al., 1994:9, Miller, 1995:340), and appear "acceptable to society" (Faderman, 1991:180). New York City DOB president Barbara Gittings tells the story of a butch who was "living as a transvestite most of her life" and when the DOB persuaded her to dress like a woman, "everyone rejoiced over this as though some great victory had been accomplished" (Miller, 1995:340).

In the 1970s, the lesbian feminists who collectively were reacting against Betty Friedan and her lesbophobic pronouncement that lesbians were a "lavender herring" (Faderman, 1991:212) continued to uphold a butch/femme exclusionary doctrine. The lesbian feminist organizations such as the Radicalesbians were mostly white, middle-class women (as was Friedan's National Organization for Women). The lesbian feminists tended to "ignore the existence of working-class lesbians" (which included most butch/femme couples), and "the vocabulary of the old lesbian subculture was usually rejected as being counter to their politics. 'Butch' and 'femme' disappeared as far as lesbian-feminists were concerned" (Faderman, 1991:219). The ideology of lesbian feminism required that women love women and women identify as women (1991:221). A butch tells the story about what happened to her one night in 1972 at a feminist meeting called "straight-gay dialogue": "I heard a voice call out, 'Are there any butches in the room?' Subconsciously, I shot my hand up. . . . 'This meeting is for women-identified women only. All butches must leave'" (Cordova, 1992:285). Butch/femme desire was considered the replication and perpetuation of heteropatriarchy and the bane of both lesbianism and feminism. Butch subjectivity was deemed self-hatred and her masculine expression was reduced to role-playing.

I consider lesbian feminist dismissal of butch/femme subjectivity a misunderstanding of the disruptive potential of female masculinity and queer femininity as well as a race and class bias. Seventies feminism preached that women should eradicate femininity, and at the same time aspire to male power without acquiring masculinity. The skewed biological determinist aspect of feminism posited femininity as a social construct enforced by patriarchy, yet left masculinity unquestioned as the "natural" effect of manhood, or a biological "fact." Enlightened men were expected to acquire the stereotypical traits of womanliness–emotional vulnerability, sensitivity, gentleness, domesticity, mothering–in order to dilute their masculinity and understand women by embodying their degradation, yet women were not supposed to embrace masculinity or phallic power in order to level the playing field.

The stone butch/femme disruption of the sex/gender system is multiple. The stonebutch successfully appropriates these traits of masculinity deemed "natural" to men–thereby denaturalizing them. The femme, by appearance and submissive desire, "should be" partnered with a biological man yet she valorizes the traits of masculinity but only on another female. As a couple, stone butch/femme replicates the binary structure of heterosexual sexual orientation, sexual practice, and lifestyle. The couple defies the rules of the sex-gender system by taking what is considered the "norm" and "natural" and queering it; as Judith Butler states, it thus "brings into relief the utterly constructed status of the so-called heterosexual original" (1990:31). Marilyn Frye says the same thing with humor when she notes that "nobody goes about in full public view as thoroughly decked out in butch and femme drag as respectable heterosexuals when they are dressed up to go out in the evening, go to church, or go to the office. Heterosexual critics of queers 'role-playing' ought to look at themselves in the mirror on their way out for a night on the town to see who's in drag" (1983:29).

The radical lesbian feminism of the 1970s has shifted towards an assimilationist agenda in the 1980s-90s that continues to repudiate stone butch/femme identity. Assimilationist lesbians, from the Daughters of Bilitis to Ellen DeGeneres, have fashioned themselves into acceptable "others" by walking the walk and talking the talk of the heterosexual mainstream, as well as by closeting their sexual practices and disavowing the dykes who foreground theirs. They have reverted lesbian identity back into the closet of Victorian "romantic friendships." Historian Lillian Faderman states, "the appeal to homosexuals to blend in had some resurgence at the end of the 1980s, which may be a harbinger of more conservative times" (1991:341, fn31). Lesbians have become a marketable target group, a commodity. Stone butch/femme on the other hand is an advertisement of queer sex. Virility and sensuousness, authority and submission, gentlemanliness and womanliness are inscribed in its aesthetics, expression, and behavior for all the world to witness. The queering of heterosexuality by the stone couple is a lucid visual representation, that is, when a stonebutch does not pass as a man and the couple is perceived as straight.

A BUTCH IS NOT BORN A WOMAN/MAN

Daddy sometimes passes unwittingly as a man, which pleases her, although she prefers to pass only momentarily and then be recognized as a queer. Daddy's attachment is to the malleable traits of masculinity, not to the biological fixity of maleness. She has no desire to walk in the world as a man and she does not desire the partnership of a heterosexual woman. Daddy says she is a butch, a female–not a woman, not a man; but in childhood, she was a "boy," not a "girl." She will tell you that she played with boys, thought like a boy, rejected girly things, and did not understand or feel comfortable with girl social interactions. After the onslaught of puberty, she mourned her androgynous body and protested against the trappings of womanhood. She was never willingly intimate with a man, and in her adult life, she never wore women's clothing. Since childhood, she watched male behavior carefully and picked the traits that she liked best. As men have, she constructed her own masculinity.

Daddy defends her masculine stonebutch identity as essential to her being, not as a "role." "Butch," and his sister "queen," "man," and "woman" are all constructed performances of gender. "Woman" and "man" are based not on a biological script but on societal expectations and paradigms that perpetuate the "norm" of aligned sex and gender expectations, that is, a male becomes a man and a female becomes a woman. A stonebutch falls out of the gender category of "woman" since "woman" does not include masculinity in its construct. That is, not without femininity pinned to it like the female bodybuilder with her hyper-masculine physique piled high above heels and bulging beneath "big hair" and heavy makeup. A stonebutch constructs her masculinity based on the models of masculinity she finds in men (and if she is fortunate, another butch), although masculinity is the antithesis of what is expected of her. She constructs her masculinity based on a need that "feels" integral and "natural" to her.

DYKE DISCOURSE

To conclude, I will return to the main title of this essay, "Toward a Dyke Discourse. . . ." Butch masculinity, femme subjectivity, and certain other queer female identities–such as those in the dyke s/m communities and transgendered female-to-males (FtMs)–do not belong in the fields of lesbian studies, feminist theory, or women's studies, all of which as I have shown valorize the category of "woman," hold power equality as an ideal, and generally disdain masculinity. Queer theory had, in its infancy, a close link to feminist theory but with a virulent anti-essentialist approach as in the work of Judith Butler. The "queer" subject was broadly defined to include a myriad of sexual orientations (even heterosexual ones), gender expressions, social constructs, deviant sexual practices, power imbalances, and anyone who fell out of the well-defined lesbian and gay constituency. It promised to always consider class, ethnicity, socioeconomics–and be global. The conundrum of queer theory is that its most useful application has been in relation to the discourse around AIDS activism (such as the work of Douglas Crimp, Cindy Patton and Leo Bersani), and for this reason has become increasingly male-focused–positing male subjectivites in its applications when it does attend to subjects at all. Female subjectivities, female bodies, sexual practices, sexualities, and dyke identity all remain undertheorized and subordinated to the male, to whom "queer" refers in the gay vernacular. For Sue-Ellen Case (1996), queer theory's evacuation of female subjectivity is in both the naming and in the privileging of the performative text over the performative body which is the foundation upon which lesbian subjectivity is built. As Case puts it, "'queer' evacuates the fulsome problematic of 'lesbian' to operate as an unmarked interpellation, thus avoiding that exclusionary specificity" (1996:15). In its non-specificity "queer" becomes a universal signifier similar to "man." Later in her book she states, "we can begin to perceive a critical axis forming along the abandonment of the term, 'lesbian' for 'queer,' in its class operations, and in its imperialistic uses, along with the evacuation of the body, as a subject-suspect" (1996:37).

Elizabeth Grosz (1995) critiques queer theory's lack of specificity and subsumption of all bodies under the term "queer" in her essay, "Rethinking Queer Subjectivity":

> A male sado-masochist does not function in the same way or with the same effect as a female sado-masochist. It does make a difference which kind of sexed body enacts the various modes of performance of sexual roles and positions. (1995:250 fn.1)

It is becoming increasingly clear that in order for radical female subjectivities, such as stone butch/femme identity, to be represented in academia, a new field of inquiry is necessary that will privilege female subjectivity; a field that will employ discourses such as autobiography, oral history, protest, performance, and testimony as well as theory, and promises to be aware of its own ramifications. It will not assume contructivism as a given but will return to an interrogation of both essentialism and constructivism, and it will regard desire and sexual practice as viable modes of identity formation.

Dyke, like queer, is a term that implies radical "in your face" identity. They are both politically weighty categories. Dyke, however, is female specific and does not carry the universally inclusive valence that "queer" and "gay" do. (Would males willingly be included in a discipline called "dyke theory" as females have been expected to find their home in "queer theory?") I still have trouble using the term dyke. By habit, "queer" slips easily off my tongue and fingers as I speak and write. But perhaps my shame at using the tough word "dyke" is reason enough to employ it and transform it into a viable new mode of study that focuses on radical female subjectivity.

REFERENCES

Bannon, Ann. *Beebo Brinker*, Greenwich, CT: Gold Medal/Fawcett. 1962, reprinted 1983. Tallahassee, FL: Naiad.

Bender, Debbie and Linnea Due. "Coming Up Butch," In Eds. Lily Burana, Roxxie, Linnea Due, *Dagger: On Butch Women*. San Francisco: Cleis Press, 1994, 96-112.

Burana, Lily, Roxxie, Linnea Due. "Introduction." In *Dagger: On Butch Women*. San Francisco: Cleis Press, 1994, 9-13.

Butler, Judith. *Gender Trouble: Feminism and the Subversion of Identity.* New York: Routledge, 1990.

Case, Sue-Ellen. "Toward a Butch-Femme Aesthetic." In Eds. Henry Abelove, Michèle Aina Barale, David M. Halperin, *The Lesbian and Gay Studies Reader*, New York: Routledge, 1988, reprinted 1993, 294-306.

Case, Sue-Ellen. *The Domain-Matrix: Performing Lesbian at the End of Print Culture.* Bloomington and Indianapolis: Indiana University Press, 1996.

Cordova, Jeanne. "Butch, Lies, and Feminism." In Ed. Joan Nestle, *The Persistent Desire: A Femme-Butch Reader.* Boston: Alyson, 1992, 272-292.

Faderman, Lillian. *Odd Girls and Twilight Lovers: A History of Lesbian Life in Twentieth-Century America,* New York: Penguin, 1991.

Feinberg, Leslie. *Stone Butch Blues,* Ithaca, NY: Firebrand Books, 1993.

Freud, Sigmund. "The Psychogenesis of a Case of Homosexuality in a Woman," In (translator unnamed) *Sexuality and the Psychology of Love.* New York: Collier Books, 1963, reprinted from 1920, 130-152.

Frye, Marilyn. *The Politics of Reality: Essays in Feminist Theory.* Freedom, California: Crossing Press, 1983.

Grosz, Elizabeth. *Space, Time, and Perversion,* New York: Routledge, 1995.

Hall, Radclyffe. *The Well of Loneliness,* New York: Doubleday, 1928.

Kennedy, Elizabeth Lapovsky and Madeline D. Davis. *Boots of Leather, Slippers of Gold: The History of a Lesbian Community,* New York: Routledge, 1993.

Miller, Neil. *Out of the Past: Gay and Lesbian History from 1869 to the Present,* New York: Vintage, 1995.

Eroticizing Safe Sex:
Pedagogy and Performance
in Lesbian Video

Christie Milliken

SUMMARY. This paper considers several lesbian-produced safe sex tapes which engage pornographic vernacular with a dual purpose, offering both a very pointed counter to the dearth of erotic imagery depicting lesbian sex/sexuality specifically by and for women, but also functioning as pedagogical (self-help) tools for rethinking safe sex. *[Article copies available for a fee from The Haworth Document Delivery Service: 1-800-342-9678. E-mail address: getinfo@haworthpressinc.com]*

In an essay entitled "The Authenticating Goldfish: Reviewing Film and Video in the Nineties," B. Ruby Rich positions the work of women artists in relation to cheaper video technologies developed around the time of the feminist sex wars in the early 1980s. This period is characterized by the polarization of the feminist movement into sharply divisive and antagonistic camps as issues surrounding the pros and cons of representing female sexuality became particularly heated in the contexts of debates involving

Christie Milliken is a PhD candidate in Critical Studies at the University of Southern California School of Cinema-Television. She is currently writing her dissertation on pedagogical sex films tentatively titled "Generation Sex: Reconfiguring Sexual Citizenship in Educational Film and Video."

Address correspondence to: Christie Milliken, 321 1/2 N. Ogden Drive, Los Angeles, CA 90036 (E-mail: amillike@scf.usc.edu).

[Haworth co-indexing entry note]: "Eroticizing Safe Sex: Pedagogy and Performance in Lesbian Video." Milliken, Christie. Co-published simultaneously in *Journal of Lesbian Studies* (The Haworth Press, Inc.) Vol. 3, No. 3, 1999, pp. 93-102; and: *Lesbian Sex Scandals: Sexual Practices, Identities, and Politics* (ed: Dawn Atkins) The Haworth Press, Inc., 1999, pp. 93-102; and: *Lesbian Sex Scandals: Sexual Practices, Identities, and Politics* (ed: Dawn Atkins) Harrington Park Press, an imprint of The Haworth Press, Inc., 1999, pp. 93-102. Single or multiple copies of this article are available for a fee from The Haworth Document Delivery Service [1-800-342-9678, 9:00 a.m. - 5:00 p.m. (EST). E-mail address: getinfo@haworthpressinc.com].

sexuality and sexual representation, pornography and censorship.[1] She argues that the "economics of video" and the conditions of viewing that it enabled, made sex and its representation more accessible to women by establishing the unprecedented possibility of safe, privatized viewing. Rich maintains

> by thus providing a new market, video also supplied the preconditions for a more diversified porn production, no longer only *with* women, but *by* and *for* them as well. Such are the contradictory results of technological atomization and privatization: our politics become more provisional, our pleasures more renewable. (emphasis in original; Rich, 1993:92)

It is in this climate of *provisional politics* and *renewable pleasure* that I want to examine issues related to sexual pleasure and the return to body politics in 1990s video practices specifically as it is *performed* in the context of several lesbian safe-sex tapes that are being widely publicized and disseminated within the gay/lesbian community.

The tapes include *Well Sexy Women* (by The Unconscious Collective, Great Britain, 1992, 50 minutes), *Safe Is Desire* (by Debi Sundahl, USA, 1993, 45 minutes) and *She's Safe!* (USA/Canada/Germany/Great Britain, 1993, 55 minutes), a compilation of shorts, public service announcements (PSAs) and excerpts from longer safe sex videos (including *Well Sexy Women*).[2] These tapes are of interest not only because they offer a very pointed counter to the dearth of erotic imagery depicting lesbian sex and sexuality within independent feature film and videomaking, but also because they have been so clearly marketed both as pedagogical (self-help) tools for rethinking safer sex *and* as erotic/pornographic entertainment.

While the majority of AIDS information in both mainstream and queer communities was originally aimed at high-risk male behavior, women have increasingly begun to produce AIDS activist video for various subcultures of women particularly at risk from the disease. In her book, *AIDS TV: Identity, Community and Alternative Video*, Alexandra Juhasz outlines the invisibility of women in mainstream AIDS documentaries and chronicles her own involvement in such projects as Women's AIDS Video Enterprise (WAVE), an AIDS prevention campaign geared to generating community-specific information made by and for low-income, minority women who are at great risk of contracting the disease. While much of this output concentrates on heterosexual risk, Juhasz applauds this alternative production as a form of "direct, immediate, product-oriented activism" (1995:1) which, in her view, is ". . . always an invitation to join a politicized community or diverse people who are unified temporarily and

for strategic purposes to speak back to AIDS, to speak back to a govern-
ment and society that has mishandled this crisis, and to speak to each
other" (1995:3).

In this context of shared self-proclaimed difference, marginality, activism and oppression, lesbians have turned to gay men not only in alliance
against those who would otherwise have ignored the crisis, but also in
order to create explicit representations of safe sex for queer women. As
Julia Creet proclaims, "From what was primarily a gay male crisis, rubber
dams, latex gloves, and condoms on cucumbers have now brought legiti-
mation and laughs to public talk about lesbian sex" (Creet, 1991:32). In a
social and cultural environment with few images of lesbian sexuality apart
from straight male pornography's longstanding tradition of lesbian sex as
a prelude to heterosexual activity, these tapes serve an important function.
By reinscribing lesbian sexuality as both personal and political (to echo an
oft-repeated phrase of 1970s cultural feminist rhetoric), these videos resit-
uate sex from strictly a private, personal realm to a fundamentally social
project.

Since these videos are relatively new, and represent what is a recent
phenomenon of depicting lesbian sex (let alone safe sex practices) in film
and video, I am particularly interested in the degree to which these tapes
borrow and *differ* from more mainstream heterosexual and gay male porn
aesthetics. The convergence of these aesthetics with those of documentary
film is another significant aspect of this work, particularly as it engages
issues of fantasy alongside the politics of sex and sexual representation of
the female body. For the purposes of this paper, however, I will concentrate on the relationships between these lesbian safe sex tapes and gay
male culture.

The alliance of lesbian safe sex rhetoric with AIDS activism has been a
complicated and problematic issue in many quarters. One of the most
contestable points about AIDS/HIV prevention within the lesbian community has stemmed from the fact that statistical evidence of woman-to-
woman transmission of HIV is relatively low. In an essay published in
Out/Look in 1992, Nancy Solomon addresses the important issues surrounding safe sex advocacy within the lesbian community. Part of the
problem seems to stem from the fact that very little medical research has
been conducted on sexual practices among women. Another problem
stems from a widespread misperception that lesbians (indeed all women)
are generally less actively interested in sex than men. For example, in the
late eighties, Dr. Charles Schable, spokesperson of the Centers for Disease
Control (CDC) argued that the center had chosen not to devote resources
to woman-to-woman transmission because: "Lesbians don't have much

sex" (quoted in Solomon, 1992:50). Lesbian activists who contend that woman-to-woman transmission is virtually nonexistent or at least highly inefficient find themselves in uneasy alliance with the staff at the CDC.

Other activists maintain that since the incidence of woman-to-woman transmission of HIV is so low, that the "propaganda" about lesbians and AIDS is a pathetic attempt at visibility. One of the complaints about *Well Sexy Women* (and tapes like it) quoted on the back pages of *Quim* is exemplary. In a letter to the editors of the magazine, a self-identified gay male contends:

> Why is it so important for lesbians that they be considered at risk from HIV? Is it because not being so makes them feel less than "full" members of the gay community? Or in the case of "butch" lesbians because it does not fit in with the male image they like to project? (*Quim*, 1994:90)

Unfortunately, this position is reflective of a common antagonism that has frequently divided members of the gay and lesbian community with respect to the AIDS crisis. It is a position which basically accuses those lesbians who overemphasize the possibilities of woman-to-woman transmission of suffering from "AIDS envy." While this phrase is indeed extremely hurtful, even pathologizing of those lesbians concerned with the possibilities of HIV transmission among women, and has no doubt motivated and enraged many, it is important to bear in mind that there is a sizable population of lesbians who also subscribe to the view that the rhetoric on woman-to-woman transmission is a form of scare-mongering which is actually conterproductive to an ethos of prosex lesbianism. Such activists include Beth Elliott and Garance Franke-Ruta (who wrote about the subject for *Off Our Backs* and *NYQ* respectively), Sarah Schulman and Robin Gorna.

In her book, *Vamps, Virgins and Victims: How Can Women Fight AIDS?* Gorna argues that it is ironically the producers of lesbian porn in the vanguard of what she calls "latex lesbianism" who have incorporated latex accessories in erotic photos and stories with far greater frequency than in gay male porn (1996:354). She remarks that "the community which has succeeded in establishing a visible, erotic, safer-sex peer norm is the community with the least need–at least in respect of the activities to which these norms apply" (1996:254). The real reason for latex lesbianism is not disease avoidance, in Gorna's view, but rather "a handy code for sexual visibility. It is a symbolism which says, 'What do lesbians do in bed? We have real sex'" (1996:354). Gorna contends that public discourse surrounding the eroticization of safer sex for men has led to a scenario in which politicians (for better or worse) talk about anal sex and State Health Authorities list information on sucking, fisting, watersports, rimming, bondage and so on. And so, she says, "lesbians want a slice of the action–after all, the boys always get more attention" (1996:352).

Rather than attempt to resolve either side of this contentious debate, the line of argument to support safe sex practices is, of course, that it is not simply a matter of HIV/AIDS, but of a whole spectrum of illnesses that can result from sexual exchange. Nonetheless, in the absence of a significant body of research to indisputably resolve the matter, safe sex advocates maintain that, at the very least, women do bleed every month, and that (however unlikely) lesbians can transmit HIV to one another through certain sexual activities, most particularly through cutting and other s/m practices. Given these facts, I would argue that a significant part of the agenda behind these safe sex tapes may indeed be less specifically related to HIV and AIDS than to the promotion of a more sex-positive, assertive view of lesbian sexuality and visibility in ways that depart dramatically from widespread views of lesbianism and lesbian identity generally promoted in the 1970s. Some commentators have suggested that in the face of prohibitive attitudes toward gay male sexuality in the light of AIDS, lesbians have picked up where gay men left off, creating an era of unprecedented sex positivity in the late 1980s and '90s. The proliferation of lesbian erotica in the past decade may be interpreted as a form of reinforcement for a sexual liberation movement severely debilitated by the right wing and AIDS, but is it also a response to the initial invisibility of lesbian sex and sexuality in the early stages of the second wave feminist movement.

It is important to note that a significant part of the standard for success in these tapes has to do with how *sexy* the actual depiction of sex is deemed to be. While this doesn't mean that the instructive or educational value of these tapes is irrelevant, most reviews of the tapes seem to concentrate more on the qualitative evaluation of the sex scenes than on how effectively or efficiently the important information allied with its practices is relayed. The fantasy of believing that this sex is somehow believably and realistically "hot" seems to be a consistent and significant part of the criteria for judgement.

For example, this marketing strategy is evident in the publicity for *Safe Is Desire* which promises "Romantic desire and club sex passion–safe sex style." In her review of the tape in *On Our Backs*, Catherine Saalfield underscores this dual strategy of education and entertainment, describing the video as "the latest, hottest and most coherent lesbian safe sex tape to date . . . Fatale's . . . romp through the romance between this interracial pair rectifies the omission from mainstream media of lesbians' experience with HIV/AIDS. It will also jump-start your girlie-engines" (Saalfield, 1993:36).

Along these lines, a quotation from a negative review of *Well Sexy Women* seems to condemn the video for its erotic/pornographic failure. Megan Radclyffe of *Time Out* is quoted in the back pages of *Quim* as saying: "This long-awaited video for lesbians, promising scenes of a 'sexually explicit nature,' has finally arrived–with more of a dull thud than a bang . . . The scenarios [sex scenes] are tepid, unfamiliar, and have trouble passing the wet test" (*Quim*, 1994:90).

It is impossible to know how these tapes are actually used/received on anything other than a case-by-case basis. Nor do I have empirical/ethnographic data to indicate whether viewers use these tapes strictly as self-help manuals to latex use and safer sex methods, as a cue to engage in sexual acts or as a form fantasy production for the viewer. Some of these issues relate to the more widespread and unresolvable debates surrounding the confusing and (often) class-based distinctions between pornography and erotica which are indeed multiple and complex.[3] Moreover, the political and representational strategies at work in sexually explicit imagery produced by women are similarly complicated, given the inherited feminist discourse about objectification. In theorizing a pornographic vernacular as a concept from which to produce better strategies for organizing communities or subcultures around safe sex, Cindy Patton argues:

> The primary goal of safe sex advocacy in a video is information, not eroticization. Although pornography might be able to provide information, the specific requirements of safe sex representation are probably at artistic odds with pornographic conventions. (1991:37)

While Patton's point is well-taken, in the context of the lesbian community, it is interesting to note that lesbian-produced safe sex videos explicitly strive to be *both* instructive *and* "sexy" at the same time. Indeed artistry seems to be the way to subsume the proselytizing aspect of the educational material contained within them.

The possible reasons for this are multiple. In part, this may be explained by the fact that women pornographers are trying to reach audiences that may be especially hostile to porn given its visibility as a target for feminist anti-porn activism and conservative crusades. Moreover, the dual influence of both the feminist and gay movements on lesbian feminism, leads to important points of convergence between lesbians and gay men in the area of sex on the one hand, and feminism's political analysis which may seem to be at odds with gay male sexual culture, on the other. Julia Creet summarizes this conflict when she states: "Our brothers have created institutions out of fantasies, while we lesbians are still arguing over whether to engage in fantasy in the first place. They have not been shy about their extensive repertoire; we need only the inclination to look" (1991:31-32). Within feminist theoretical (especially film theory) paradigms that have problematized the whole notion of *looking* in the first place, the explicit representation of sex in lesbian safe sex video practices may be read (and rendered more acceptable), under the rubric of necessary instruction.

Julia Creet argues that a gay male influence is clearly present in recent depictions of lesbian sex, citing examples from *On Our Backs* and the work of the Kiss & Tell Collective. In her essay "Lesbian Sex/Gay Sex: What's the Difference?" she argues that larger numbers of gay men and lesbians recognize themselves as "sharing political or sexual proclivities" (1991:32), being careful to point out that this doesn't mean that lesbians and gay men are necessarily doing the same things. What emerges instead, says Creet, "is perhaps the first commonly shared homoerotic language. 'Fisting,' for example, can involve very different parts of the anatomy for men and women, yet when understood in homoerotic argot, it speaks of a sameness in practice" (1991:32).

Appropriation from gay bar/back room culture is presented in *Safe Is Desire*. To convince Dione of the importance of safe sex practices, Allie takes her to a sex club which offers a peer education performance by the Safe Sex Sluts. After the demo (which includes one woman dressed as a nurse who first instructs, then participates in explicit safe sex activity on stage with two other performers), the couple ventures upstairs to a "back room" where an orgy is in progress. This scenario presents a spectrum of sexual orientations/activities with slapping, strapping, spikes, studs, leather, tattoos and piercings. Catherine Saalfield states that there is even what she calls "lesbian faggotry" presented as one butch leans over to suck another butch's dick/dildo (Saalfield, 1993:36).

Two of the shorts included on *She's Safe!* employ similar tactics: *Jill Jacks Off* (1993, 3 minutes) and *Girls Will Be Boys* (1993, 3 minutes) made by Texas Tomboy (a.k.a. Heidi Deming). In *Jill Jacks Off*, a woman with a short crew cut dances to club music in front of a mirror in a bedroom and slowly strips off a frilly dress to reveal her combat boots, strap-on harness and leather gear. As she continues to dance, apply a condom to her dildo and "jack off," another butch (in a suit and tie) is shown spying on her (with binoculars) through her bedroom window. This short clearly incorporates elements of gay male iconography in terms of dress codes. Stylistically this is accomplished through fast cutting, highly stylized lighting techniques, stop and slow motion photography and the use of club music (as opposed to synchronous sound). This creates a sense of sexual energy which constitutes the tape and its message as fashionable and "in the know." It also mobilizes interesting issues related to voyeurism and exhibition (long associated with the male gaze and female performance) that are reappropriated here from a woman's point of view.

These sequences highlight a gender-bending performativity of sex and may also be read as a parody of gay male porn conventions which (often) centralize sexual performance around the penis. I ally this with gay male porn rather than straight (which also privileges a male sexual narrative around the genitals) because the butch-butch pairing here clearly has more in common with same sex tropes than with heterosexual conventions. Julia Creet speculates (and these tapes seem indicative of this) that gay men have become fetishized sex symbols for many lesbian sexual fantasies, as she states: " . . . butch-butch sexuality is easily fed by images of two men doing it. Because gender-bending is a time-honoured tradition in queer culture, it makes our imaginary crossings of sexual boundaries perhaps predictable in the more fluid realm of fantasy" (1991:31).

Creet goes on to point out that AIDS activism (in which lesbians have played a significant role) and safe sex discourse have also provided a shared language and forum for lesbians and gay men. Gay-lesbian rapport, in fact, is a repeated theme in *Safe Is Desire*. For example, when Allie and Dione are making their way to the bedroom on their first date, Allie's gay roommate comes running out of his bedroom and begs her for a condom (he has run out). Allie chastises him, but quickly pulls one out of her purse in ready supply. This tape shows her roommate's "trick" and the trick's hard on (which is certainly unusual in a *lesbian* safe sex tape) with deliberate nonchalance. It is precisely the kind of graphic representation of the overlapping between lesbian and gay male culture for which Catherine Saalfield lauds this particular tape most (Saalfield, 1993:36).

In keeping with Ruby Rich's assertion of the more provisional politics characteristic of this third wave feminist moment (cited at the beginning of this paper), these safer sex videos for lesbians may be seen to employ self-conscious and exhibitionistic strategies to build a lesbian audience that perceives itself in a sexual vanguard for women. This includes images of lesbians appropriating phallic objects and sexual role-playing in an attempt to rewrite female sexual pleasure as specific and local, instead of essential and universal.

A gay male influence is only part of what comprises lesbian sex representation, since lesbian imagery develops in several directions, some closer to existing forms and structures, and others more divergent. Of course, the lesbian community can hardly be defined as a sexual community to the degree that, say, the gay male community has. But in the absence of a longstanding tradition of women-produced sexual imagery, one could argue that these tapes–generated under the sobering discourse of the HIV/AIDS epidemic–actually function, simultaneously, as a celebration of lesbian sex. In other words, while they function under the rubric of a pedagogical agenda seeking to advise lesbians on safe sex practices, perhaps these tapes accomplish something else as well.

To educate about safer sex means to address the variety of ways in which women–including lesbians–are sexual. In this sense, these tapes blur the epistophillic tendency aligned with nonfiction film's educative function by simultaneously engaging the scopophilic pleasures of viewing long associated with feminist film theory's masculinist spectatorial paradigm. Perhaps, indeed, the *pleasure in knowing* and the *pleasure in seeing* are not so very far apart. As Diana Fuss puts it, if seduction is, after all, a question of transport–not of moving in space but of moving the desires of another person–and bonds of identification provide the critical channels of this transport, then ". . . perhaps the mimetic function of the educational process is precisely what invokes, impels, or institutes desire, which is to say that all pedagogy comes under the sign of sexuality. The question is thus not, When does a scene of instruction become a scene of seduction? but rather, When is a scene of instruction not a scene of seduction?" (Fuss, 1995:126).

Alongside the proliferation of lesbian porn, dyke bars with back rooms, high profile sex radicals and overall of a more erotically charged lesbian scene both in mainstream culture and in queer communities, these lesbian safe sex tapes offer an unprecedented variety of sexual choreographies. In the myriad ways in which lesbians may identify–including (however provisionally), positions of race, class, age, ablebodiedness and ethnicity–reconceptualizing identity politics without abandoning it altogether is part of the challenge of contemporary concerns. Beyond their strictly informative value with regard to safe sex practices, these tapes may be seen as pedagogically valuable for any woman grappling with identity and sexuality in a culture that polices and represses both.

NOTES

1. This debate has been discussed at length in various texts. Most notably, the Barnard Conference in 1982 entitled "The Scholar and the Feminist IX" represents a pivotal moment in the public staging of the debate between the rather clumsily labelled pro-sex/anti-censorship and anti-pornography/pro-censorship divide. Many of the essays and issues presented at the conference are collected in *Pleasure and Danger: Exploring Female Sexuality*, edited by Carole S. Vance.

2. As a curated package of woman-to-woman safer sex videos, PSAs and

excerpts, *She's Safe!* is the first-ever program of its kind, proceeds from the sale and rental of which benefit the Erotic Video Education (EVE) Fund, a San Francisco-based funding source supporting production of woman-to-woman safe sex erotic videos.

3. The degree of sexual explicitness will not be presumed to be a mark of distinction between the erotic and the pornographic in tapes which also aim to visually (and often explicitly) instruct women on safe sex practices. As Richard Fung argues, "since convincing people to practice safe sex is the currently favoured AIDS prevention strategy, this necessitates promoting the pleasure of sex in itself by depicting it in a more or less explicit way" (356). Indeed, the line between what is sexually explicit and what is pornographic is a line that many have sought to draw but few have done so adequately. The only line that gets mass agreement is that porn tends to be bad art.

REFERENCES

Creet, Julia. "Lesbian Sex/Gay Sex: What's the Difference?" *Out/Look* #11 Winter 1991: 29-34.

Fung, Richard. "Shortcomings: Questions About Pornography as Pedagogy." In *Queer Looks: Perspectives on Lesbian and Gay Film and Video.* Eds. Martha Gever, John Greyson and Pratibha Parma. Toronto: Between the Lines Press, 1993: 355-367.

Fuss, Diana. *Identification Papers.* New York: Routledge, 1995.

Gorna, Robin. *Vamps, Virgins and Victims: How Can Women Fight AIDS?* (New York: Cassell, 1996).

Juhasz, Alexandra. *AIDS TV: Identity, Community and Alternative Video.* Durham: Duke University Press, 1995.

Patton, Cindy. "Visualizing Safe Sex: When Pedagogy and Pornography Collide." In *Inside/Out.* Ed. Diana Fuss. New York: Routledge, 1991, 373-386.

Quim, Issue #5, 1994.

Rich, Ruby. "The Authenticating Goldfish: Re-Viewing Film and Video in the Nineties." In *1993 Biennial Exhibition.* Ed. Thelma Golden, John G. Hanhardt and Lisa Phillips. New York: Whitney Museum of Art, 1993, 86-99.

Saalfield, Catherine. "Review of Safe Is Desire." *On Our Backs.* September/October, 1993. 36.

Soloman, Nancy. "Risky Business: Should Lesbians Practice Safer Sex?" *Out/Look* #16 Spring 1992: 46-52.

Vance, Carole S. Ed. *Pleasure and Danger: Exploring Female Sexuality.* New York: Pandora Books, 1984, Reprinted 1992.

Women on the Edge of a Dyke-otomy: Confronting Subjectivity

Myra J. Hird

Jenz Germon

SUMMARY. This paper considers some of the contradictions of authenticity as a defining feature of lesbian community in Aotearoa/ New Zealand. We sketch the genealogy of marginalization within the lesbian community through the development of subjectivity, community and political struggle for equality. To this end, we deconstruct three major, interrelated "problems" in speaking of lesbian politics: subjectivity, community and universality. At its broadest, the lesbian subject refers to any woman who desires women. But in practice such a "continuum" does not satisfactorily identify a bounded community. In articulating its voice, any community necessarily creates a governing discourse, thereby creating outsiders and insiders to that community. This paper explores the conditions under which the lesbian community has marginalized an "other" lesbian subject with particular reference to sexual practices and associations

---

Myra J. Hird holds BA, BSW, and MSW degrees and completed a DPhil at Oxford University before taking up the position of Lecturer at Auckland University. Dr. Hird lectures in the areas of research, gender, feminist theory and sexuality. Her forthcoming book on violence, *Women, Men and Violence: From Childhood to Adulthood* is published by Polity Press.

Jenz Germon holds a BA in Sociology at the University of Auckland and is currently completing a Masters degree in Sociology in the area of intersexuality.

Address correspondence to: Myra J. Hird or Jenz Germon, Department of Sociology, University of Auckland, Private Bag 92019, Auckland, New Zealand.

[Haworth co-indexing entry note]: "Women on the Edge of a Dyke-otomy: Confronting Subjectivity." Hird, Myra J., and Jenz Germon. Co-published simultaneously in *Journal of Lesbian Studies* (The Haworth Press, Inc.) Vol. 3, No. 3, 1999, pp. 103-111; and: *Lesbian Sex Scandals: Sexual Practices, Identities, and Politics* (ed: Dawn Atkins) The Haworth Press, Inc., 1999, pp. 103-111; and: *Lesbian Sex Scandals: Sexual Practices, Identities, and Politics* (ed: Dawn Atkins) Harrington Park Press, an imprint of The Haworth Press, Inc., 1999, pp. 103-111. Single or multiple copies of this article are available for a fee from The Haworth Document Delivery Service [1-800-342-9678, 9:00 a.m. - 5:00 p.m. (EST). E-mail address: getinfo@haworthpressinc.com].

with heterosexuality in order to establish an authenticity of identity. *[Article copies available for a fee from The Haworth Document Delivery Service: 1-800-342-9678. E-mail address: getinfo@haworthpressinc.com]*

INTRODUCTION

Current debates in both academia and lesbian communities suggest that what may have begun as a declaration of desire and love for women is far more complicated. Whilst essentialists maintain that behind all superficial transformations of lesbians exists a fundamental bodily desire, constructionists view all identities as performed, practiced and subject to change depending on historical and social contexts (Stein, 1992). Recent academic pre-occupations with postmodernism suggest that identity is nebulous, flexible and context-dependent. If the subject is dead, then so too the lesbian? The following paper inquires into some of these current debates and their possible consequences for a lesbian subjectivity in the Aotearoa/ New Zealand context. This paper will focus on debates concerning sexual practices and association with heterosexuality to focus on particularly relevant and volatile aspects of lesbian identity. We want to explore the theoretical map drawn by a diverse group of scholars, which articulates a formation of political identity dependent upon boundaries, marginalization and both the promise and unattainability of liberation. That is, this paper hopes to chart the fundamental paradox of all communities defined by shared social identity, that marginalization is both necessary to the maintenance of that community and preventive of liberation.

LESBIANISM IN AOTEAROA/NEW ZEALAND

Once upon a time a lesbian identity related specifically to a woman's sexual desire for other women and "sexual practices" per se were left uncritiqued. The development of lesbian-feminist scholarship and a political movement signified the woman-identified-woman: a woman subject to the two-fold oppression of sexism and hetero-sexism. The genealogy of the lesbian community in Aotearoa/New Zealand has followed a similar path to the rest of the Western world–albeit in a slightly different time frame. This section outlines a number of key developments of lesbian political culture from the 1960s through to the 1990s.

In the first attempt to organize politically, a group of lesbians advertised in a Wellington (Aotearoa/New Zealand's capital city) newspaper in 1963, calling for interested women to join the *Radclyffe Hall Memorial Society* (Laurie, 1991:76). Eight years later the first lesbian club opened in Auckland. Developed out of an informal underground of predominantly working class and Maori (indigenous) women, it represented an explicitly lesbian community (Glamuzina, 1993:14). Lesbians were actively involved in many of the early initiatives of the Women's Liberation movement, including: abortion rallies, founding women's centers and rape crisis services. In mid-1974, *Sisters for Homophile Equality* (SHE) collaborated with socialist and feminist women to open a center that was to become the forerunner of the Women's Refuge (Glamuzina, 1993).

Over time, established codes of conduct and notions of *lesbian* began to be challenged by women whose exposure to women's liberation was shaping a different concept of lesbian identity. As the numbers and influence of feminist lesbians grew, the perceived takeover by this "new wave" created resentment. Moreover, the tension underpinning the relationship between lesbian and heterosexual feminists came to a head at the 1977 United Women's Convention. A group of lesbians demanded the inclusion of lesbians in the official line-up of speakers and a ban on male media. Conflict continued to be a feature of feminist conferences in 1978 and again in 1979 (Eagle, 1978; Glamuzina, 1993):

> [S]ome of us had firmly established our need for lesbian separatism. We found that so often when we met in Women's Liberation groups our women energy was dissipated because so much of that time was being taken up in considering men. (Eagle, 1978:8)

The 1977 convention inspired the formation of a lesbian feminist theory group–*Lesbians Ignite Fire Brigade*. The focus of political activity was on visibility, typified by Lesbian Pride weeks. A *Lesbian Mothers Defense Fund* was initiated in 1980 to assist lesbian mothers with custody battles. Gay Liberation was founded in Auckland by Maori lesbian and activist Ngahuia Te Awekotuku in 1972 (Glamuzina, 1993:34). The longest running lesbian feminist journal, *Circle*, began in 1973 and continued until 1985. Over time, many women within that organization became dissatisfied with the seemingly reformist and conservative political focus of many gay men. A separatist politic gathered momentum.

Lesbian practice was not subject to the same types of erasure by the law in Aotearoa/New Zealand as elsewhere. The 1961 Crimes Act criminalized sexual contact between an adult woman and a woman under the age of sixteen. Unsurprisingly, lesbians were active in the enormous rights campaign that resulted in the introduction of the Homosexual Law Reform Bill to Parliament in 1985, that dealt with three specific issues: anti-discrimination; decriminalization and equal age of consent. The introduction of the Bill polarized the nation: a petition organized in opposition to the Bill was widely disseminated and supported by church groups, conservative politicians and numerous public figures. The anti-discrimination clause was ultimately defeated, the amended Bill entering the statutes in July 1986. Six years later sexual orientation finally became incorporated into human rights legislation as grounds for protection from discrimination (Auckland Lesbian and Gay Lawyer's Group, 1994:96).

Currently, political activity has re-focused on rights, this time in relation to marriage. In 1996, three lesbian couples sought a declaratory judgement, claiming discrimination in contravention of the Bill of Rights. This claim has inspired considerable debate amongst lesbians. Some perceive that legal sanction of same-sex marriage will protect property and inheritance rights. Others contend that embracing the normative institution of heterosexuality represents a form of cultural assimilation. This debate represents one aspect of the opposition to the association between lesbianism and heterosexuality, a central point we will explore further in the following section.

MARGINALIZATION IN THE LESBIAN COMMUNITY

Whilst the 1970s are commonly acknowledged as an era of a separatist politic in North American lesbian culture (Faderman, 1991:273), in Aotearoa/New Zealand fervent separatism was still very much alive, well into the late 1980s. In the past two decades some of the most acrimonious attacks by separatists have been toward other lesbians rather than men. The first form of attack has been directed towards lesbians who in some way "associate" with men. Those lesbians who desire to marry, women who sustain relationships with men, mothers of male children, and those living with heterosexual women have been accused of "collaborating with the pricks" (Ruston, 1986). The second form of attack concerns "acceptable" sexual practices. Bisexuality, sado-masochism and the "mimicry" of heterosexual sex (in the use of, for instance, dildo) has been cause for the delineation of the *real* lesbian from the faux. An analysis of literature during this period provides some insight into both the "collaboration with heterosexuality" problem and the veracity of the intent to separate "genuine" from "pretend lesbians." For instance, Julia Penelope (1996) accuses lesbian-identified women who do not *look like lesbians* as "the enemy":

> The essence of The Feminine consists of a repertoire of facial expressions, gestures, body postures, and ways of moving–silent lan-

guage of acquiescence, of yielding, that signal DANGER to the Dyke. I say "danger" because she is a likely betrayer, someone who wants to conform to the demands of male society. (1996:132-3)

Penelope goes on to list "external signals of acquiescence" that will identify *the enemy*. Beware the lesbian who wears any of the following: "dresses, skirts, and blouses, make-up, high heels (*anything over a 1/2 inch*), plucks her eyebrows, has longish to long hair, and adorns herself with certain types of jewellery–pearl necklaces or diamond broaches" (1996:129, italics our emphasis). The hostility directed toward women who identify as bisexual and so-called "lipstick" lesbians centers around the notion of *passing*–passing for straight (association with heterosexuality) and thus benefiting from the privileges of heterosexuality. At the 1987 Lesbian Festival a woman in the process of coming out was denied entry to a dance, illustrating the rejection of lesbians deemed "inauthentic" because of the perceived association with heterosexuality. In addressing this issue, Rankine (1987) suggests that exclusion inevitably becomes a "slippery slope":

> [T]his kind of policing and this dilemma about who we "let in" will be with us as long as we restrict our definition of lesbians. . . . Pakeha [Maori term for non-Maori] middle class women are more likely to fit these notions of what "real lesbians" are, because we don't have such obvious common ground with our men against structures that oppress us both. (1987:6)

Although not as prevalent as it once was, policing at lesbian events continues, with women's authenticity being challenged at the door of Auckland's annual Lesbian Ball as recently as 1996.

With regard to sexual practices, the 1990s have seen the emergence of an insider/outsider configuration particularly focused on the delineation of "genuine" lesbian sexual practices that exclude bisexuality, straight sex and sado-masochism. Each of these sexual practices is considered to allude, at least to some extent, to gender identity, revealing the root of the attack: the association between sexual practice and heterosexuality. Bisexuality directly involves men and by "sleeping with the enemy" bisexuals invite criticism by not choosing exclusive relationships with women. A myriad of sexual practices defined as "straight sex" also invite criticism. The use of dildos, the degree of assertiveness/aggressiveness when having sex and vaginal penetration are a few of the sexual practices which are regulated in the unending requirement to exclude all that is (or might be) heterosexual from the lesbian. Nor is it surprising that the practice of sado-masochism is considered to represent regimes of violence against women, given that much of the traditional rhetoric of radical lesbians has centered on "lesbian healing" and the desire to develop a pure lesbian *self*.

DECONSTRUCTING LESBIAN IDENTITY

Behind lesbian feminist discourses which seek to separate lesbians from straights through the bodily desire (exclusively for women) is a reduction of gender to sex and sex to the body. This reduction has consequenced a strategic definition of a bounded identity of the "lesbian." This strategy has seemed reasonable; indeed, hardly a strategy at all. For how can we deny that subjectivity is constructed and practiced on the body. Indeed, according to feminist materialism, there is no pre-body subjectivity (Rose, 1996).

However, the problem with "the body" as the base site of subjectivity is that it rests on an overly simplistic conflation of the natural and the social. Focus on the body leads to an overemphasis on differences *between* sexes as opposed to *within* sexes (Spelman, 1988). Little attention has been paid to how differences within each sex/sexuality might shape experiences of subjectivity. The very fact that current debates focus on the "authenticity" of various sexual practices for lesbians reveals that there are indeed many different ways of actualizing sexual desire. Women who identify as lesbians come to understand, speak about and judge themselves, at least in part, as particular beings with a particular identity. That is, lesbians engage in a constant process of subject-ing themselves as lesbians (Rose, 1996). These subjectivities are not only products of language; in much more concrete ways "lesbian" is about comportment (how to walk, how to sit), artifacts (Doc Martin boots, jeans, sweaters), spaces (bedrooms, clubs, restaurants, the street), and objects (picket signs, rainbow flags, etc.). It is also about sexual practices: most fundamentally, how the fulfillment of desire and pleasure are sought.

LESBIAN IDENTITY AND POLITICAL STRUGGLE

Whilst community is an understandable dream in a world that despises and devalues many different types of "other," such a dream is problematic because differences within any group tend to become suppressed in the interests of social cohesion (Fuss, 1989; Young, 1990; Gamson, 1996; Yeatman, 1993; Card, 1994). The ideal of community de-temporizes a conception of social life by setting up an opposition between authentic and inauthentic identities. The desire for unity creates a hierarchical opposition whereby any moves to define an identity always depend on excluding some, in order to separate the pure from the impure; the real from the false; the authentic from the inauthentic (Young, 1990:300). Any definition or category creates an inside/outside distinction, and the logic of identity operates to keep such boundaries firmly drawn:

> [t]he systems of morality that we rely upon valorize authenticity. Humans have come to relate to ourselves as psychological beings, possessing an inner self, one that is authentic and true, that holds the secrets of identity and against which we measure the extent to which we are leading an authentic life. (Rose, 1996:22)

A counter-discourse demands freedom to pursue and express pleasure in whatever form it takes. In this view, prohibitions against, amongst others, bisexuality and sado-masochism belong to a history of "repression and oppression against *sexual deviants*" (Card, 1994: xvii). The expectation that our sexualities should be clearly marked and easily read is premised on this notion of authenticity representing "an internalizing of the state's desire that we have our identity papers ever in order, and take up the work of policing our own conceptions of what constitutes a legitimate sexual minority" (Lehring, 1997:192).

The paradox of social movements is that the categories on which social movements are based are, at the same time, both oppressive and the source of political power. Most social movement theory has assumed that identities are already formed, are stable, and become visible through political organizing and struggle (Gamson, 1996). Most identity politics is both strategic (what works) and constitutive of a power struggle (who gets to say what lesbians are). But it is more than these things: it is a struggle to identify who "we" are. The discourse sustained by cultural feminism, on the one hand, sets the limits of our struggle for equality by reducing "lesbian" to a finite and bounded number of signifiers. On the other hand, we do not see the forest for the trees if we only see "identity" as the site of oppression (Seidman, 1993). The lesbian movement was predicated on very real, institutional and individual discrimination to which collective struggle was the only viable way forward.

A possible way out of this apparent quagmire rests in our understanding of subjectivity and political struggle. Lesbians need to re-visit the basis on which lesbians have been identified and limited as a particularity. The practice of lesbianism, and what it means to be a lesbian, is varied and diverse. Lesbian subjectivity based on corporeality results in an overly simplistic and reductive identity which excludes many lesbians through both silencing and/or her subjection to a psychology of "deviance."

We can use the unstable and assembled subjectivity to political advantage. We might see politics as that space which exists between established policy and any group's claims for equality (Laclau, 1995). In making a claim for equality, we have identified "lesbian" as a particularity based on a specific set of signifiers. But we have other options. We might base a claim on a more complex notion of particularity, based on a more inclusive definition of oppression. Furthermore, particularities are not fixed, nor do they have to exist outside of this political moment. In this paper we throw in our hats to giving up the search for an essential lesbian identity and concur with Haraway's (1990:198) suggested response to fragmentation: coalition based on affinity rather than identity. This is a unity "without . . . appropriation, incorporation (or) taxonomic identification" *sans* domination and incorporation.

CONCLUSIONS

In articulating the voice of "lesbian" as a particular configuration of signifiers, we have not only excluded all lesbians who "deviate" from these signifiers but also defined what counts as experience of this subjectivity. The "authentic" lesbian in Aotearoa/New Zealand has been most recently involved in debates about sexual practices and associations with heterosexuality. We have identified that the tendency to link lesbian identity and political struggle is teleological: "we have an identity and therefore a politics" (Fuss, 1989:100). Lesbian political movements have been built on assumption of an essential fixed natural essence: that is, a subjectivity premised on an exclusive desire for women actualized in particular sexual practices. In such an essentialist model, successful resistance and political gains are seen to depend on a clear classification of collective identity (Gamson, 1996:396). We suggest in this paper that whilst a definable and fixed "lesbian identity" may be a strategic and useful political tool, its danger in excluding and further fragmenting lesbian subjectivity needs to be recognized. This tension may be seen as an opportunity to further de-stabilize gender. Lesbians who do not "fit" the subjectivity required by the lesbian community may experience exclusion but also create a potential space for de-stabilizing and disordering this community. As Flax remarks:

> If we do our work well, "reality" will appear even more unstable, complex and disorderly than it does now. In this sense, perhaps Freud was right when he declared that women are the enemies of civilization. (1987:643)

REFERENCES

Auckland Lesbian and Gay Lawyers Group. *Out Law: A Legal Guide for Lesbians and Gay Men in New Zealand*. Auckland: Auckland Lesbian and Gay Lawyers Group Inc., 1994.

Card, Claudia. *Adventures in Lesbian Philosophy*. Bloomington: Indiana University Press, 1994.

Eagle, Allie. "Lesbian feminism in action." *In Circle*: 8-11, 1978.

Faderman, Lillian. 1991. *Odd Girls and Twilight Lovers: A History of Lesbian Life in 20th Century America*. New York: Columbia University Press.

Flax, Jane. "Postmodernism and gender relations in feminist theory." *Signs* 12:621-43, 1987.

Fuss, Diana. *Essentially speaking: Feminism, nature and difference*. New York: Routledge, 1989.

Gamson, Joshua. "Must identity movements self-destruct? A queer dilemma." In *Queer Theory/Sociology* edited by Steven Seidman. Oxford: Blackwell Publishers, 1996, 395-420.

Glamuzina, Julie. *Out Front: Political Activity in Aotearoa 1962 to 1985*. Hamilton: Hamilton Lesbian Press, 1993.

Haraway, Donna. "A manifesto for cyborgs: science, technology, and socialist feminism in the 1980's." In *Feminism/Postmodernism* edited by Linda Nicholson. London: Routledge, 1990, 190-233.

Laclau, Ernesto. "Subject of politics, politics of the subject." *Differences*: 7:146-164, 1995.

Laurie, Alison. *Parker & Hulme: A Lesbian View*. Auckland: Auckland Women's Press, 1991.

Lehring, Garey. "Essentialism and the political articulation of identity." In *Playing With Fire* edited by Shane Phelan. New York: Routledge, 1997, 173-198.

Penelope, Julie. "Passing lesbians: the high cost of femininity." In *An Intimacy Of Equals: Lesbian Feminist Ethics* edited by Lilian Mohin. London: Onlywomen Press, 1996, 118-149.

Rankine, Jenny. "Letter to the editors." In *Lesbians In Print* 11:3-7, 1987.

Rose, Nikolas. *Inventing Our Selves: Psychology, power and Personhood*. Cambridge: Cambridge University Press, 1996.

Ruston, R. "Lesbian separatism is vital to all lesbians." In *Lesbians In Print* 7:28-34, 1986.

Seidman, Steven. *Queer Theory/Sociology*. Oxford: Blackwells, 1996.

Spelman, Elizabeth. *Inessential Woman*. The Women's Press: London, 1988.

Stein, Edward. *Forms of Desire*. New York: Routledge, 1992.

Young, Iris Marion. "The ideal of community and the politics of difference." In *Feminism/Postmodernism* edited by Linda Nicholson. New York: Routledge, 1990, 300-323.

Sticks and Stones

Sally Abrahams

SUMMARY. "Sticks and Stones" is an exploration of life-in-the-ghetto; twenty five years of sex and politics, and wrestling with sexual correctness. It is concerned with the changing paradigms of lesbian 'vice and virtue': the butch-femme bar girl; the feminist woman-identified-woman; the sex radical warrior; the chic babe who's Queer and Here. How's a lesbian supposed to find an identity in all that? And remain true to her erotic preferences and sexual practices, frequently in the face of severe opposition? Joan Nestle, Gayle Rubin, Emma Healey and Sue O'Sullivan act as critical guides through this retrospective view of my collisions with erotic orthodoxy; they add discursive weight to the recollected experiences of negotiating historical shifts and re-alignments in ideology and practice of (Western) lesbian sexuality. Is the only way to spot a 'real' lesbian to watch what she does in bed? *[Article copies available for a fee from The Haworth Document Delivery Service: 1-800-342-9678. E-mail address: getinfo@haworthpressinc.com]*

I've been called some names in my time. Endearments and insults, classifiers and qualifiers. Some I've picked up and pinned proudly to my

Sally Abrahams is an Australian writer and holds a BA in Communications from the University of Technology, Sydney, where she majored in Writing and Textual and Cultural Studies. An active, if somewhat agnostic, member of the sisterhood, Sally aspires to be a thinking girl's lesbian. For the last decade Sally has worked with women affected by childhood sexual abuse, and is presently engaged in a Master's program in Rehabilitation Counseling at the University of Sydney. She writes poetry after midnight.

Address correspondence to: Sally Abrahams, P.O. Box 214, West Gate, NSW 2048, Australia.

[Haworth co-indexing entry note]: "Sticks and Stones." Abrahams, Sally. Co-published simultaneously in *Journal of Lesbian Studies* (The Haworth Press, Inc.) Vol. 3, No. 3, 1999, pp. 113-122; and: *Lesbian Sex Scandals: Sexual Practices, Identities, and Politics* (ed: Dawn Atkins) The Haworth Press, Inc., 1999, pp. 113-122; and: *Lesbian Sex Scandals: Sexual Practices, Identities, and Politics* (ed: Dawn Atkins) Harrington Park Press, an imprint of The Haworth Press, Inc., 1999, pp. 113-122. Single or multiple copies of this article are available for a fee from The Haworth Document Delivery Service [1-800-342-9678, 9:00 a.m. - 5:00 p.m. (EST). E-mail address: getinfo@haworthpressinc.com].

chest; other less appealing appellations I've batted hard back to their source. But this latest epithet has a nasty smell to it. Rotted, sticky, slimy. Mud dredged from the depths, flung with unerring hostility. Beneath the stated word, now bouncing about the room, I hear the whispered threats. Blasphemy and sacrilege! Begone from the temple. Unclean. Unclean.

Ouch. Another unfavourable review. It shouldn't surprise me. I'm a career lesbian, been fucking girls since I was thirteen, but I've never been a good lesbian. As the definitions swirled and eddied around my body, I've never quite managed to conform to the rules. I've failed the test, yet again. Ex-communication from the Lesbian Nation looms.

When I first attached the Lesbian label to my barely budding breast I thought the worst name-calling would come from the mouths of hetero-sexuals. Lemon. Queer. Pervert. Frustrated, ugly, sick. Sinner. It was 1970 and "the word *lesbian* still conjured up images of misery and depravity" (Healey, 1996:1). The wicked kind of woman my mother warned me about. However, once embraced, the attractions of lesbian life did out-weigh, convincingly, any perceived threat of slander and disrepute. Board-ing school made it easy. After all, adolescent curiosity in a dormitory might just be a passing phase. And beyond the school walls, rebellion was in the air. The rule of the fathers was being disturbed. The sons and the daughters, the women and wives, were revolting against the assumptions and stereotypes. Words and meanings were being reshuffled.

Unfortunately, my Headmistress was impervious to such stirrings and I was expelled, sent back to my country town. In disgrace. A small rural community in the early seventies was not quite the place to flaunt a lesbian lifestyle. With a firm hand on my closet door, I camouflaged myself with indifferent heterosexual liaisons, crossed days off my school years: 12 November 1974–final exam; 13 November 1974–caught the train to Sydney, found a room in a hostel, and went looking for a ghetto I knew had to exist. It's a well-trodden path. "Dissident sexuality is rarer and more closely monitored in small towns and rural areas. Consequently, metropolitan life continually beckons to young perverts. Sexual migration creates concentrated pools of potential partners, friends, and associates. It enables individuals to create adult, kin-like networks in which to live" (Rubin, 1984:295). I found Chez Ivy, the back bar at the Cricketers' Arms, the Glebe HQ of Campaign Against Moral Persecution. And love. The closet abandoned, I took up Camp.

By the time I walked into my first meeting of Sydney University Femi-nists in 1977, the influence of feminism and "the development of lesbian politics . . . meant that 'lesbian' [had become] generally recognised as a self-conscious sexual identity, a choice rather than a biological perversion" (Ashton, 1996:164). It's true, I didn't go looking for political enlightenment. My motives were more carnal than cerebral. As a new student without a single acquaintance on campus, I'd figured the best place to find other lesbians would be at a feminist meeting. After all, everyone knew feminists were just a bunch of radical lesbians, and everyone was right. Liberation from the well of loneliness. The room was full of noisome hairy-legged dykes advocating anarchy and revolution. I was hooked. I picked up one of the green and purple badges lying on the table, found a seat near the door and settled in to listen. I chose to become a lesbian feminist.

Sitting here now, once more denounced, I wonder, briefly, what on earth possessed me? My collisions with orthodoxy, as I've attempted to navigate the historical shifts and re-alignments in ideology and practice, have been myriad. As Gayle Rubin says in her essay, *Thinking Sex*, "The sexual system is not a monolithic, omnipotent structure. There are continuous battles over the definitions, evaluations, arrangements, privileges, and costs of sexual behaviour" (1984:294). Hunting through my history–that of Western, English-speaking lesbians–I find a place littered with the torn banners and bloodied manifestos of such battles. From the butch-femme paradigm of the first sixty years of this century through the feminist woman-identified-woman of the 1970s, to the sex radical warrior of the 1980s, and now the chic babe who's Queer and Here in the 1990s–the Nation has had a turbulent time.

Much effort has been directed to determine the "correct" way to be a lesbian. This has more often than not been focused on what we do with our bodies. In *Lesbian Sex Wars*, Emma Healey (1996) traces the changing "fashions" in lesbian sexuality and the pitched battles which have been fought over the sexual body of the lesbian. How do we define the lesbian? Is she a woman who has sex with women or a woman who does not have sex with men? Is a lesbian necessarily a feminist? Is a feminist necessarily a lesbian? How have various sexual practices been viewed by lesbians, and in what ways have these practices been used to both include and exclude the practitioners from the Lesbian Nation? Healey argues that "in the last twenty years or so we have not been content to accept [our] diversity, rather we have wanted to create a single, acceptable template of how to be a lesbian in a heterosexual world" (1996:3). She is also concerned that "rather than reconciling ourselves to the various strands of our own history, we make enemies of it. Yesterday's courageous pioneer is tomorrow's *bête noire*, yesterday's political radicalism is tomorrow's political fascism" (1996:2).

Indeed, as a young truly revolutionary lesbian I was aware that butch-femme was a pitiable reactionary mimicking of heterosexuality. I knew it was Ideologically Unsound. The notion that butch-femme relationships might be "complex erotic statements, not phony heterosexual replicas . . . serving both as a conspicuous flag of rebellion and as an intimate exploration of women's sexuality" (Nestle, 1996:90) was not to be entertained. False consciousness for sure. But late at night, when all good folk were abed, we ruffled our skirts, tucked our tuxedos and called it fancy dress fund-raising. Rhetoric be damned, we liked the aesthetic. Joan Nestle, an American historian and unrepentant fiftysomething femme, commented in 1987: "The irony of social change has made a radical, sexual political statement of the 1950s appear today as a reactionary, nonfeminist experience" (1996:91). Irony plus—a decade on, and I watch as butch-femme realises itself as the preferred *post*-feminist performance.

My own failure to match the variously determined codes has invited a barrage of criticism from the sisterhood. It was particularly perilous in the 1970s for a lesbian like me. I tried hard. It was said that feminism was the theory and lesbianism the practice. But mine never quite lined up. I wore overalls and flying boots to all the demonstrations and marches; dragged my lover from the back of the police vans; sprayed *Lesbianism When Only The Best Will Do* on the Tempe overpass; danced for Emma Goldman: I earned my stripes. But I had secrets. I lived in fear of any of my comrades discovering the (shamefully unburned) black lace bra under my slogan-emblazoned T-shirt. I covered up my male-identified shaved legs, hid my razor—that sharp edged tool of the patriarchy—in my underwear drawer.

The stumbling block was the fact that I'd been a lesbian before I was a feminist, and I'd acquired some bad sexual habits. Before I knew they were wrong. It was obvious I needed to Raise my Consciousness, but neither weekly CR sessions nor intensive study of feminist tracts eradicated my desire for patriarchal, unequal sex. Lying side-by-side caressing the wetness was simply not my style. Further compounding my difficulties was the fact of my engaging in a monogamous relationship. Definitely no-go: this aping of heterosexuality and heterosexual oppression. "Nonmonogamy was a challenge to patriarchal assumptions about female sexuality" (Healey, 1996:70). Fortunately, my treason was remedied when my girlfriend engaged in the true struggle and acquired a couple of extra lovers.

Still, I was suspect. White, middle class, Jewish, fond of my bourgeois father, not averse to my sisters' heterosexuality. In a ghetto where the personal was political such ingredients were not promising. My socialist credentials were shaky, my feminist fervour was dubious, my sexual practice was politically precarious, and, in an era when all good revolutionaries vociferously supported the Palestinian struggle, my surname gave rise to sideways glances from those who believed all Jews to be Zionist. The vanguard was a tough place to be. I started losing my grip on feminism. Not on the feminism that spoke of all women's right to autonomy, equal pay, abortion, freedom from violence, sexual and otherwise. More and more though, the feminism speaking about lesbianism, as spoken by lesbians, started slipping away from me.

At the end of the 1970s a lesbian feminism emerged which theorised a transformation of lesbianism "from a stigmatised sexual practice into an idea and a political practice that posed a challenge to male supremacy and its basic institution of heterosexuality" (Healey, 1996:29). All very well, but it did leave a few feminists, those who didn't want to kiss their sisters, out in the cold, fucking with the enemy and propping up the patriarchy. Not a problem. In 1979 the Leeds Revolutionary Feminists defined a "political lesbian as a woman-identified woman who does not fuck men" (Healey, 1996:65). Lesbian feminism thus created a definition of lesbianism which had nothing whatsoever to do with lesbians or lesbian sex. "It was rather like marketing engine oil as washing powder" (Healey, 1996:31). *"Any woman can be a lesbian,"* went the words of the song, and she doesn't even have to get her fingers wet. It may have been an effective recruitment ploy to swell the ranks of the Lesbian Nation but, for me, the severance of practice and theory at the point of sex, in the articulation of sexuality, has a disturbing tendency to radically de-sexualise the experience of lesbianism. Life in the ghetto was getting confusing.

Sue O'Sullivan, a British veteran of the "sex wars," in her collection of essays, *I Used To Be Nice*, argues that identity politics, whilst giving substance and voice to varied women, may "in an unravelled world of meanings . . . come to grief and confusion . . . [because] fast on the heels of those fabulous feelings of identity certainty . . . came the discordant calls of deviation or distinction, leading, in its most fractured and absurd stages, to hierarchies of oppression which soared higher and higher as newly delineated differences were claimed and named" (1996:141). The exploration of these differences was too often bypassed and difference became "the be-all and end-all, frozen into rigid identities, no longer located within social relationships and the possibility of change or alliance" (1996:141).

At the same time, this fragmentation saw the totalising world view that feminism offered to some, mainly white, women, crack open, as "a multitude of identities defined lives, loyalties and political correctness" (O'Sullivan, 1996:194). Which banner to march under on International Women's Day, which float for Mardi Gras? Should one even parade at Mardi Gras?

The eighties arrived and the ghetto was awash with feminisms and lesbianisms jostling for supremacy as *the* defining, authentic politic. The most ferocious hustling took place in the bedroom. Suddenly the lesbian bed became public space and it was obvious that more than a few of us had been breaking the rules. And this time we were not going to get away with it. Whereas in the 1970s my foibles and agnostic approach to ideology were points of contention, they were now viewed as subversive and grounds for expulsion.

One of the dominant feminist projects at the time concerned itself with the sexual and physical violence and exploitation experienced by women at the hands of men. Like many of my sisters, I thought this project was long overdue, but a curious thing happened on the floor of the forum. Gayle Rubin points at the phenomenon. "A good deal of current [1984] feminist literature attributes the oppression of women to graphic representations of sex, prostitution, sex education, sadomasochism, male homosexuality, and transexualism" (1984:302). She asks, "Whatever happened to the family, religion, education, child-rearing practices, the media, the state, psychiatry, job discrimination, and unequal pay?" (1984:302). In the meeting places and magazines, in the academies and bars, the agent of oppression had been identified and she wore a leather jacket. The SM dyke–the enemy within–had arrived.

Not only was SM a "manifestation of men's power and violence against women," it was also "an inherently fascist (and racist) practice" (Healey, 1996:100). SM was also something real lesbians didn't do. I knew as soon as I opened the pages of *Coming To Power* (1982), an obscene collection of essays and erotica by Samois (a group of self-declared perverts in San Francisco) that the Lesbian Nation was headed for war. There would be no neutral ground. Vanilla or not. And definitely no seats on the sidelines. "Often debates around SM degenerated into simple name calling with both sides often using the same names. Thus you could be labelled a fascist for opposing SM or be guilty of fascist behaviour by practising SM" (Healey, 1996:10). Sheila Jeffreys, lesbian feminist and vanilla vigilante, called for "revolutionary" Consciousness Raising about SM and lesbians. But, as Healey points out, "Discussion was possible as long as everybody understood from the beginning who was right and who was wrong and who would have to change" (1990:91).

Unfortunately, my proclivities proved resistant to erotic cleansing and so I ran away to Paris–where the wearing of black leather jackets was *de rigeur*, regardless of sexual practice, and the rules of *la boudoir* less austere, more indulgent of the perverse and theatric. One weekend, in search of fluent conversation and a supply of English language books, I ventured across the Channel to London. In support of the sisterhood, I made my purchase from a feminist bookshop, but when I mentioned to the hitherto friendly assistant I thought I'd pursue some interpersonal chat at the London Lesbian and Gay Centre, she thrust a leaflet into my hand. Produced by LASM (Lesbians Against SadoMasochism), it was unambiguous. "Warning. Do not go to the London Lesbian and Gay Centre unless you are prepared to be in an environment which is rife with fascists, racists, misogynists and sadomasochists" (O'Sullivan, 1996:211). An invitation one could hardly refuse.

I must have picked a slow night. LASM would have had more luck at a Conservative Party convention, but of course those brave lassies knew the most important targets were their black booted sisters and no amount of condemnation was too great. One woman did accost me, disturbed by my "Nazi uniform" of studded belt, leather jacket and boots. My attire, which some less perceptive observer might have read as my slavery to fashion, my penchant for punk, was for her an obvious sign I was anti-Semitic. That's OK, I replied, I once was a Zionist. On further exchange I learn she's a Gentile with very many best Jewish friends and I tell her I'm glad to see the *goyim* are looking after me.

Everyone knew what was best for me. Censorship, in the interests of protecting ourselves from ourselves, was deemed right and necessary. The early issues of *Bad Attitude* and *On Our Backs* (American lesbian-produced magazines full of irreverent and salacious articles) were not easy to track down. Few bookstores would stock them because "the contents were found to be prosadomasochistic, antifeminist, antiwoman, anti-Semitic, and racist." And as Joan Nestle reminds us "you all know, these are the words that call for exile from our community" (1996:138). It was the cold of a European winter which drove me back to Sydney rather than my reading habits, but I soon learned it was prudent to keep one's copies of *Wicked Women* magazine under the bed. At least until one had ascertained the preferred position of each new bedroom visitor. How do you like your sex, sweetheart? With or without aberration? One's reputation depended upon it.

The blessed healing haze of hindsight reveals it was ludicrous, such assaying of political and personal integrity by virtue of some perceived predilection for specific sexual behaviours. Penetration was a point of contest. Healey reports: "It is often said that all lesbian feminists were fundamentally opposed to penetration" (1996:74). My experiences would tend to contradict that, but maybe I was just lucky. It's certainly true that phalluses started popping up everywhere. "Dildos, strap-ons, butt plugs, pornography and vibrators. These were a few of their favourite things.

Through the reclaiming of the phallus and, by implication, fucking, SM broke the spell of vanilla lesbian essentialism just by giving women willies–literally and metaphorically–and, in so doing, offering them the plurality of identification . . . lesbians were at last able to experience themselves as a multiplicity of identities" (Ashton, 1996:170). Holes were appearing in the lesbian body. Demands were made for lesbians to choose their flavours and woe betide those who preferred rocky road. By the time the dust started to settle in the late 1980s, I'd about sworn off ice cream completely. Then Queer came along and everyone had to get fucked.

Trust me to choose the heady free-for-all orgiastic years of Queer to try a little celibacy. In a ghetto where the road to revolution was the root, a sex-less life was tantamount to treason. Queer Nation, land of sex and sin, turned off the electric fences (O'Sullivan, 1996:113), opened its borders and urged all transgressives to come taste the thrill of the forbidden. "Queer . . . repossessed such outdated notions as SM and butch/femme. Butch and femme have been stripped of their lesbian identities and been turned into sexual positions. SM, . . . cleansed of its old contentious definitions of violence and abuse, . . . has been re-modelled as a healthy, sexy alternative to a repressive vanilla sex mentality" (Healey, 1996:193). Erotic evangelism swept the ghetto. I comforted myself with the thought that chastity in the age of Queer had its own peculiar transgressive qualities, and waited for the wheel to turn. It was clear Queer would disappear sooner rather than later. Reliant on the "fun of being dangerously transgressive, [it forgot] that, by our very natures, most lesbians and gay men are practised transgressors anyway" (Healey, 1996:193). The appeal of the outlawed, the naughty is undeniable. And yet, I wonder. "Once the wickedness is recognised and aspired to by others, is it really wicked?" (O'Sullivan, 1996:116).

And then Cindy Crawford shaved k.d. lang on the front page of *Vanity Fair* and I'm so cool and so chic I don't need any theory. Although, if Julie Burchill is right in declaring "a designer dyke isn't any old muff diver . . . to be in with the invert crowd you must be beautiful, powerful, rich or famous" (Ashton, 1996:158), then I've missed the boat again. In her essay, "Getting Hold of the Phallus: 'Post-Lesbian' Power Negotiations," Charlotte Ashton writes of the "new broader definition of lesbianism–post-lesbianism . . . being negotiated in and through the mainstream media" (1996:158). She goes on to suggest that "following the impact of post-modernism and its burying of the biological lesbian, the battleground has shifted to the arena of iconography and aesthetics" (1996:163). The babes of the nineties are too hip for rhetoric, too chic for politics. They stay away from the F word. "Post-lesbianism . . . in this all-new, all-singing, all-dancing, all-fucking, all-phallic leather'n' lipstick form has given lesbian-ism an unprecedentedly positive profile" (Ashton, 1996:172). But it's been bad press for feminists.

"The so-called loony, ugly (read not stereotypically feminine) lesbian, increasingly designated as an arbiter of rigid political correctness, remains a figure of derision and hatred, especially whenever the *politics* of femi-nism or lesbian feminism become a contentious issue in the larger soci-ety" (O'Sullivan, 1996:116). The choice is obvious. Feminist frump or lesbian chic. "So post-lesbians have adopted traditional signifiers of femi-ninity, to distance themselves from the time-honoured butch look. With big hair, short skirts, lipstick and lycra, post-lesbians are holding up a mirror to the mainstream and reclaiming the components of 'passing' as totems of transgression. This is the Revlon revolution, Sister!" (Ashton, 1996:163). Ashton is quick to point out that "the problem with holding a mirror up to the mainstream is that usually the mainstream fails to appreci-ate the irony. It simply sees itself—its own codes, its own concepts, its own kind" (1996:172).

I wonder if the mainstream sees what the lesbian is doing to the phallus. Healey suggests in the "growing 'dildo' culture" of the 1990s, the dildo has become "less of a male penis and more of a female one" (1996:194). Judith Butler, who is proof that "lesbian feminist" has not become an oxymoron, theorises this appropriation: "The task, then, is not simply to disjoin the Phallus from the penis, but to underscore the Phallus as a transferable property, . . . an *incitement* to substitution and proliferation, such that modes of penetrability and penetration, control and submission, are properties which are fundamentally plastic and transferable" (1992:164). Is Butler performing the archetypal lesbian-as-castrator here? The detachable penis, rescued from the triple curse of impotence, prema-ture ejaculation and one-shot wonders, is transmogrified. The flesh made silicone. "The dildo . . . can represent the lesbian colonisation of male power, or the lesbian's control of her new, burgeoning sexuality. Once the tool of the patriarchy, the penis has become the weapon of a lesbian sexuality that plays patriarchy at its own game" (Healey, 1996:196). For less than $40, any dyke can whip out her rubber bullet and wreak havoc among the plutocrats, shatter the hegemony, puncture patriarchy. Quite an achievement. Now if I could only remember where I put mine . . .

The theory/praxis conjunction is a hazardous knot to tie. Joan Nestle wrote in 1987: "I suggest that the term *Lesbian-feminist* is a butch-femme relationship, as it has been judged, not as it was, with *lesbian* bearing the emotional weight the butch does in modern judgement, and *feminist* be-coming the emotional equivalent of the stereotyped femme, the image that can stand the light of day" (1996:96). I would suggest that in less than a decade these meanings have been reversed. Now, it's the feminist carrying the can. My adolescent nieces boast to their school mates about their lesbian aunty, but they don't mention I'm a feminist in case their friends get the wrong idea. In case they think I am politically correct. Which of course I've never been.

Which is why I've been handed the dunce hat again. But this time I ain't wearing it. Call me what you like. Fluff-rubber, man-hater, ugly as a hat full, bitter and twisted. Worse than the torturers of Chile. I've heard it all before. Dodging the slings and arrows comes with the territory. However, the latest barrage of names surprises me. After twenty years of unadulterated devotion to the cause, I thought I'd get away with it.

Heterosexual, she called me, *traitor, heretic*! Names I have no inclination for. Because I'd entertained a man, in private so to speak, to an intimate degree. Caught dancing with the devil. And he wasn't even gay, so it wasn't properly queer. You'd think I would've learned by now. The only way to spot a Real Lesbian is to watch what she does in bed. I will recite to myself: *Mea culpa. How I fuck is always more important than why.* But the lesbian label, muddied and frayed, is here to stay. It's a name I have a taste for.

REFERENCES

Ashton, Charlotte. "Getting Hold of the Phallus: 'Post-Lesbian' Power Negotiations," Nicola Godwin et al. (eds), *Assaults on Convention*, Cassell UK, 1996, 158-177.

Butler, Judith. "The Lesbian Phallus and the Morphological Imaginary," *differences: A journal of Feminist Cultural Studies*, 4.1, Indiana University Press, USA, 1992, 133-171.

Healey, Emma. *Lesbian Sex Wars*, Virago Press, UK, 1996.

Nestle, Joan. *A Restricted Country*, New York: HarperCollins, UK, 1996.

O'Sullivan, Sue. *I Used To Be Nice*, Cassell, UK, 1996.

Rubin, Gayle. "Thinking Sex: Notes for a Radical Theory of the Politics of Sexuality," Carol Vance ed., *Pleasure and Danger*, New York: Routledge and Kegan Paul, USA, 1984, 267-319.

Samois. *Coming to Power*, Boston: Alyson Publications USA, 1982.

Lesbian Sexual Renegades?

Julie Inness

SUMMARY. Whereas gay men have idealized the gay man as a sexual renegade, lesbians often are eager to distance themselves from practitioners of "deviant" lesbian sexuality. This paper explores how "acceptable" lesbian desire has been articulated in terms of a vision of "normal" sex that reflects feminine norms, making much of lesbian sex literally and figuratively unspeakable–yet also creating a potentially radical fringe of lesbian sexual outlaws. *[Article copies available for a fee from The Haworth Document Delivery Service: 1-800-342-9678. E-mail address: getinfo@haworthpressinc.com]*

Hot Stud. Handsome, well-endowed submissive bottom wants to meet masculine, hairy, butch top. Like wrestling and uniforms.

Aware Vegetarian. Kind, caring gay woman seeks sincere and warm partner for walks, reading and cuddling. Like cats and theater.

Opening the pages of a major gay publication to the personal advertisements, it is glaringly apparent that lesbians and gay men often yearn for different ideals, at least in public. While gay men commonly mention the size of their penises and go into loving detail about their sexual fetishes, lesbians typically discuss their hobbies, pets and career aspirations. Miss-

---

Julie Inness is Associate Professor of Philosophy at Mount Holyoke College. Her research focuses on ethics and feminist theory.

Address correspondence to: Julie Inness, Mount Holyoke College, Philosophy Department, South Hadley, MA 01075.

[Haworth co-indexing entry note]: "Lesbian Sexual Renegades?" Inness, Julie. Co-published simultaneously in *Journal of Lesbian Studies* (The Haworth Press, Inc.) Vol. 3, No. 3, 1999, pp. 123-132; and: *Lesbian Sex Scandals: Sexual Practices, Identities, and Politics* (ed: Dawn Atkins) The Haworth Press, Inc., 1999, pp. 123-132; and: *Lesbian Sex Scandals: Sexual Practices, Identities, and Politics* (ed: Dawn Atkins) Harrington Park Press, an imprint of The Haworth Press, Inc., 1999, pp. 123-132. Single or multiple copies of this article are available for a fee from The Haworth Document Delivery Service [1-800-342-9678, 9:00 a.m. - 5:00 p.m. (EST). E-mail address: getinfo@haworthpressinc.com].

123

ing from many lesbian advertisements is mention of everything from sex toys to cherished sexual fantasies, feathers to feet, dildos to uniforms. Whereas gay men have idealized the gay man as a sexual renegade, lesbians often seem eager to distance themselves from the practitioners of "deviant" lesbian sexuality. How has sexuality been socially constructed so as to make many lesbians feel uneasy viewing themselves as sexual renegades or experimenters? Has this construction affected lesbian desire? In this paper, I explore how "acceptable" lesbian desire has been articulated in terms of a vision of "normal" sex that reflects feminine norms, making much of lesbian sex literally and figuratively unspeakable–yet also creating a potentially radical fringe of lesbian sexual outlaws. I conclude by considering whether gay men's discussion of sex has anything valuable to offer lesbians, especially in its promotion of fantasy.

On initial consideration, it seems that gay men and lesbians would accept radical sexual ideas since both groups are already seen by society as "sexually deviant." Having sexual contact with someone of the same sex automatically makes one sexually unorthodox, with utter disregard for the particularities of how one is having sex with the partner. From society's perspective, lesbians remain sexually radical whether they use their fingers for sex or dildos, just as gay men are deviants whether they engage in anal or oral sex. Given that they are already seen as sex radicals by society, we might guess that lesbians and gay men would easily embrace sexual radicalism in their own lives. This, however, has not proven to be the case for many lesbians, something apparent from personal advertisements.

Personal advertisements are undeniably varied. The advertisements written by those living in New York City may differ from those written from a small town in the midwest. Advertisements written by gay men sometimes mention nothing about sex; advertisements from lesbians sometimes talk about nothing but sex. Advertisements in erotic publications differ from those in news ones. For the purposes of this paper, I do not attempt to do justice to this variety. Rather, I use passages from a small selection of advertisements to provide a motivation for my exploration of common foundational assumptions about lesbian sexuality. (The content of the personal advertisements I discuss is a composite of a number of individual advertisements; sources I drew upon include advertisements in Boston's *Bay Windows*, Hartford's *Metro*, the national *Advocate*, and Western Massachusetts' *The Valley Advocate*.) I believe that looking closely at a handful of personals and thinking deeply about what they reveal can lead us to understand fascinating things about how we theorize sex in our society. Lesbian personals suggest that the interest shown in radical sexuality by a subpopulation of lesbians, especially lesbians located in major urban areas, is not permeating all lesbian self-representation across the country; as Arlene Stein writes, "the growing visibility of lesbian-made representations of lesbian sexuality, and the rise of a sexual fringe, may be more indicative of the fact that a sexually active vanguard is becoming more visible than that such attitudes and practices are trickling down to the grass roots" (Stein, 1993:33). Rather than pursuing an empirical study of lesbian sexual behavior, I pursue a theoretical exploration of some of the underlying reasons and arguments that could lead lesbians to disavow forms of radical sexuality, leading them to view the "sexually active vanguard" with suspicion. My goal is to explore whether they are reasons to believe that rejecting sexual talk and fantasy may be harmful to lesbian desire.

> *Ready for anything. Everything goes. Oral service. Seeking well hung male. Passive bottom. Men in uniforms. Jocks. Want to play cowboys? Teddy bears only. Greek service. Older men. Younger men. Foreskin enthusiast. Circumcised only. Like leather? Tit play. Construction workers welcome. Mutual J/O. Wanted hairy top. Smooth guys. Want a man who is clean shaven with a mustache.*

Reading over gay male personals, the richness and heterogeneity of the sexual imagery is apparent. Many gay men display no hesitation in describing the sexual practices they favor or the physical characteristics they find stimulating. The writers of these ads accept that they will be understood and accepted by gay male readers.

The gay male personal advertisement descriptions are striking for several reasons. They display a nuanced and complex language for conveying specifics about sexual desire; gay men have ready access to an exceptionally broad range of words to communicate with others about sex, a vocabulary consisting of hundreds of words. The advertisements also reveal that many gay men are comfortable with sexual fantasy; the parameters of eroticization include everything from feet to uniforms. A sexual fantasy is not something to be hidden, but something to be specified in advertisements so that one can find another willing to play a role in it. As Richard Mohr puts it, gay men are able to create through fantasy sexual persona that, for example, combine the erotic excitement of "soldiers, sailors, aces, punks, lumberjacks, hardhats, roustabouts, truckers, carnies, and stevedores" (Mohr, 1992:167). A gay man can bring together "a pirate's earring, a biker's tattoo, a gladiator's cuff, a policeman's cuffs, a cowboy's hankie, and engineer's boots" (Mohr, 1992:167) into a sexual fantasy that subverts the authority of these roles due to their fantastical combination. Through fantasy, gay men embrace their ability to recreate the boundaries of their own sexuality, refusing to be confined to an essentialist notion of sex.

> *Looking for a friend. Sense of humor. Enjoy romance. Cuddling at night. Seeking someone who can hold my hand. Ready for warmth, kindness and sincerity? Sensuous woman. Many hobbies and interests. Like backrubs and deep conversations. Seeking someone for nights by the fireplace. Cute femme. I want to find a special friend.*

Although some personals by gay men and lesbians are undeniably similar, in general lesbians often are reticent about sex within personals. Many advertisements fail to mention sex altogether, mentioning instead the writer's desire for "caring," "warmth" or "friendship." The sexual body of the advertisement writer comes close to vanishing; lesbians seldom refer to the size of their breasts, specifics about their genitalia or details about other erogenous zones. Instead of mentioning desired sexual practices, lesbians often use sanitized words such as "sensuous," "back rubs" or "cuddling." Even when lesbians mention specific characteristics such as "cute femme" that could be understood as conveying sexual content, the language is often clearly sexually defused. "Cute femme" comes to mean a woman who performs "feminine" tasks at home such as cooking, not a woman who likes a specific role in sex. In place of discussion of favored sexual practices or fantasies, lesbian writers of personals admit to such acceptable feminine preoccupations as character compatibility and romance; fantasies about contented relationships displace fantasies about sex.

Reflecting upon some lesbian personals, it appears that lesbians and gay men have access to different linguistic resources when it comes to sex. In contrast to the rich terminology of many gay men, lesbians often use a much more limited range of words to "talk sex" with one another. Whereas gay men have slang terms to convey such sexual nuances as someone who is sexually excited by big, old or hirsute men, lesbians have none. When a gay man states in a personal ad that he "has nine inches," other men realize that he is referring to his penis; if a lesbian were to state that she "has thirty five inches" or "has one inch," the typical lesbian reaction would be puzzlement and the sincere question, "of what?" If a lesbian says she is "well hung," confusion is once again called for–is she discussing her breasts or genitalia? Why is she mentioning the size of either? When a gay man makes it clear that he is looking for a "smooth man," he conveys that he is seeking a man who lacks body hair. If a lesbian states that she is looking for a "smooth woman" she conveys little sexual meaning. In all of these cases, the lesbian's message collapses as a sexual one.

Given this linguistic scarcity, lesbians have recourse to words such as "cuddle" and "rub," words that may convey a generalized physicality and, hence, sexuality, but that fail to convey the full heat of sexual desire. Lesbian personal advertisements reveal that lesbians find it challenging to find the words to describe lesbian desire. Even the word "sex" becomes fraught with difficulties: ". . . 'lesbian sex' was so foreign a term it was practically phallic. Drop the 'lesbian' and it wasn't much better. . . . if my girlfriend said the S(ex) word, I'd place my index finger over her lips, gently commanding silence" (Roy, 1993:6).

As I have mentioned, gay male personal advertisements reveal that gay men relish sexual fantasy, participating in what Richard Mohr calls "a creative adorational playfulness" (Mohr, 1992:167). Men casually admit that they can be sexually excited by uniforms or jockstraps, older men or younger men, body hair or its lack–the world is seen as full of potential sources of sexual pleasure, pleasure that individuals can realize through active construction of sexual fantasies with others. Yet lesbians in personals are often reluctant to publicly embrace sexual fantasy. Rather than, for example, stating a desire to meet older or younger women, lesbians typically state that they seek women their own age (in which case their own age is not thought to convey a particular sexual predilection). Lesbians say little about whether they long to touch small or large breasts, embrace women who are teachers or carpenters, have sex in public or open fields, or make love with women dressed in denim or lace. This silence about sexual fantasy in many lesbian personals bears with it the suggestion that lesbians do not need such fantasy; there is some sort of "pure" lesbian sex that is sullied by fantasy.

Underlying gay male advertisements, there is an idealization of sexual rebellion, an ideal most readily available to men. Not surprisingly, the picture of lesbian sexuality that I have discussed is deeply rooted in traditional assumptions about femininity. The fact that lesbians lack a rich language with which to discuss all the nuances of lesbian desire is not surprising in a world where women are discouraged from talking about sex as "not something good girls talk about" (whereas men are encouraged to talk about sex, albeit heterosexual, if they are to merit the accolade "real men"). Stereotypically, that gatherings of women are supposed to focus on everything from clothing to the possibilities of romance with specific men, but the gatherings are not to include conversation about, for example, the sexual prowess of the women present. A culture in which women fail to talk sex–even to the extreme of not telling heterosexual husbands after decades of marriage whether or not they are having orgasms–is hardly one which encourages lesbians to talk sex. If sex is seldom mentioned, there is no reason to imagine that lesbians will have a rich language of sexuality to invoke.

Sexual fantasy is also something traditionally discouraged for women. Despite a specialized market of erotica for women, there is nothing comparable to the overwhelming amount of popular culture that encourages men to engage in sexual fantasy, including erotica, pornography, commercials, movies, music. In conversation with other men, men are encouraged to think about the specifics of their own desire (as well as being exposed to the sexual stories of other men). Women, in contrast, are seldom encouraged to have sexual self-knowledge; instead, they are expected to focus their attention on what their male partners need for their own satisfaction. Women are also expected to be passive in sexual activity. Actively fantasizing is a violation of this expectation. Neither commercials, movies nor songs encourage women to ask themselves about sex, "what would I like today?" Quite the reverse is true: nice girls don't think about sex any more than they talk about it. Given that women are actively discouraged from fantasizing, it comes as little surprise that lesbians are often reluctant to link themselves to sexual fantasy.

Is there any harm if many gay men cast themselves as sexual James Deans while lesbians typically cast themselves as sexual June Cleavers? The sexual language of gay men might be dismissed as politically undesirable, revealing nothing more than an excessive masculine obsession with sex. The paucity of sexual language for lesbians could be seen as politically progressive; this is especially true in a world in which male and female homosexuality is so readily understood as "only about sex." By distancing themselves from sex talk, we might argue that lesbians establish themselves as beings who lead complex lives outside of the bedroom, not "sexual deviants."

As a political strategy, however, rejecting sex talk is a failure. Not only do hostile heterosexuals "read" sex into lesbian behavior no matter how apparently innocent of sexual content, but, even more harmfully, silence about sex is more likely to harm than enable lesbian desire. As Camille Roy notes, ". . . soon the self-imposed and culturally imposed silence become a strain. Eventually, the body and language intersect" (Roy, 1993:6). Silence or near silence about sex is a strain for lesbians because it involves continual self-denial; rather than acknowledging and exploring a desire, the desire must be denied hearing by others.

We might argue that a rich vocabulary for lesbian sexuality is unimportant because what matters is actual lesbian behaviour; lesbians may have a sparse sexual vocabulary, yet still pursue a wide range of sexual behaviour. As philosophers of language such as Benjamin Whorf have argued, however, language shapes what we are capable of thinking or imagining: ". . . a language is not merely a reproducing instrument for voicing ideas but rather is itself the shaper of ideas, the program and guide for the individual's mental activity, for his analysis of impressions, for his synthesis of his mental stock in trade" (Whorf, 1980:114). Our language shapes what it is possible for us to think about or imagine; "we cut nature up, organize it into concepts, and ascribe significances as we do, largely because of . . . language" (Whorf, 1980:114). Lacking the words for sex limits what we can imagine and, hence, put into practice. Sexual language is prior to the possibilities of behavior. A wild and varied sex vocabulary offers lesbians a way to create their desires as well as communicate them to others. As Camille Roy writes, putting words to sex is a form of improvisation, a creation of new possibilities, an active process of remaking desire: "this sexual dialect has a quality of improvisation. It is urban. Unsettling. Undoing. An expressive explosive moment–understanding words of sex in relation to my body" (Roy, 1993:11).

But it is not enough for lesbians to talk sex–fantasy is also needed. Whether gay men discuss varied sexual scenes they wish to act out, participate in drag or dress themselves up as an impossible combination of cowboys, construction workers and college boys, they are establishing themselves as authors of their own sexual scripts. In these cases, sex becomes not something that is given, but something that needs to be "acted out." Sex is transformed into something that depends upon not only the individual's imagination, but often also his ability to respond to another's imagination. Just as children learn to think about varied possibilities of life choice by dressing up, gay men discover through fantasy that they have the choice about what elements to bring together in sex. When lesbians deny themselves fantasy, they deny themselves adult versions of dressing up and storytelling. By hearing stories, acting out stories, and dressing up, children learn that they are their own story tellers, capable of selecting different paths and having varied adventures. By engaging in sexual fantasy, lesbians locate themselves as creators of their own ever-changing sexuality, learning that they can change guises and have varied adventures when it comes to sex. Whether dressing up with a dildo and jock strap or acting out a torrid scene with a construction worker by the ocean, lesbians learn that their own imaginations can control sex. As Minnie Bruce Pratt writes, "if I can ask for touch, I can ask myself to do anything I want" (Pratt, 1995:70).

Acting out a story or dressing up with other children, children also learn how to be responsive to others, learning to pay attention to what other children add to the common story, discovering how to respond to another child's boredom, frustration or different interests. Although sexual fantasy might seem to alienate lesbians from one another, leaving sexual partners focused on the fantasy rather than each other, this need not be the case. Ideally, sexual fantasy requires and teaches responsiveness. The lesbian dressing up with a dildo and jock strap needs to discover how her partner responds to the dildo and jock strap. She needs to pay attention to cues from her partner, learning how she signals excitement or boredom. Just as improvisational theater demands the closest of mutual attention from those engaged in it, sexual fantasy between partners demands that partners be aware of one another and capable of communicating.

Sexual fantasy is always potentially subversive. As Teresa de Lauretis explains, ". . . representation in the external world is subjectively assumed, reworked through fantasy in the internal world and then returned to the external world resignified, rearticulated discursively and/or performatively in the subject's self-representation—in speech, gesture, costume, body, stance, and so forth" (308, de Lauretis). As de Lauretis notes, sexual fantasy allows lesbians to take the world and rework it, changing meanings in the process. The meaning a lesbian gives to her speech, gesture, costume, body and stance can be wildly different from the meaning attached to her speech, gesture, costume, body and stance in the dominant social world. When, for example, a lesbian can take a dildo and use it on another woman, have the other woman use it on her, then take it off altogether, the dildo certainly stops being a "simple" representation of a male penis. When a lesbian wears a man's coat and briefs, taking them off to reveal her female body, she is not simply "trying to be a man." When a lesbian fantasizes about being submissive to her partner, it does not mean that she necessarily wishes to be submissive in her everyday life. Sexual fantasy is a reworking of desire that allows for questioning or rejection.

The uneasiness of many lesbians with talk about sex and sexual fantasizing has contributed to the "outlawing" of certain lesbians; lesbians engaged in butch/femme or s/m relations have been pushed to the periphery of "acceptable" lesbian sexuality. Although the reasons for this outlawing are undeniably extremely diverse, including political debates about the acceptability of such practices, one crucial reason is that both butch/femme and s/m lesbians often violate the implicit code against sexual talk and fantasy. In the past decade, both butch/femme and s/m lesbians have become increasingly vocal about sex, openly discussing the norms of their sexual subcultures. Furthermore, both butch/femme and s/m lesbians implicitly and explicitly challenge lesbian fear about sexual fantasy. Seeing a lesbian dressed in butch or leather regalia is a clear challenge to anyone who thinks lesbians should avoid such fantasy. But perhaps all lesbians have something to learn about talking and fantasizing sex from the groups that are marginalized by other lesbians. As Camille Roy writes, "whether butch or sadomasochism or extremes of gender–what can't be represented is the locale for invention and exchange" (Roy, 1993:11). S/m practition-ers, for example, are comfortable experimenting with sexual scenes as well as building a language to discuss the specificity of their desires. As Arlene Stein writes, "s/m embodied sex as performance . . . providing an endless supply of fantasy images, and a gendered archetype for the sort of erotic tension required by the emerging model of lesbian sex" (Stein, 1993:31). Butch/femme lesbians have also constructed language to cap-ture their desires–not only the terms "butch" and "femme," but also words such as "stone" and "kiki." Butch/femme lesbians must also en-gage with sexual fantasy in the process of determining what it means to be butch or femme in bed on any given day. If lesbians wish to learn how to talk and fantasize about sex, they can enter into a dialogue with those they have pushed to the sexual margins, for those at the edges often see things missed by others. As Minnie Bruce Pratt writes, "As for whether fucking makes a woman straight, I say that when two women do it, the act *can* get considerably bent" (Pratt, 1995:107). If we are to create a rich language for sexuality, it is vital that we talk with each other in the lesbian commu-nity since language needs to be able to communicate to others. It is not sufficient to take a copy of JoAnn Loulan's *The Lesbian Erotic Dance* (1990) and retreat to the privacy of the bedroom, for the creation of a shared language demands publicity.

Lesbians often look askance at gay male sexuality, viewing it as politi-cally regressive rather than progressive, understanding it as embodying the worst aspects of masculine sexuality. But this paper suggests that all les-bians, not only those on the sexual periphery, have something to learn from gay male representations of sexuality. As Arlene Stein writes, lesbian sex renegades have already started exploring the sexual possibilities of gay male culture: "Drawing on the iconography of prefeminist lesbianism, gay male culture, and heterosexual porn, this lesbian sexual fringe introduced a new vocabulary of lesbian desire, a world of dildos and harnesses, butch and femme, tops and bottoms, lust and intrigue" (Stein, 1993:32). By exploring how gay men playfully combine and recombine their sexual fantasies, creating words in the process to express their de-sires, lesbians may discover that talking and thinking sex is a source of personal energy, an arena that allows for individual self-creation and free-dom. As Richard Mohr suggests, gay men discover through their sexual fantasies how to "work through" their oppression, transforming and sub-verting the status quo through envisioning things from a gay male perspective: ". . . liberation is to be found in a working through of past oppression, a working through in which the constituents of oppression become morally diffused by being incorporated into and transformed in the self-creation of an oppressed minority's development of a positive [sexual] ideology of and for itself" (Mohr, 1992:172). Similarly, lesbians can discover in their sexual fantasies a way to rethink power rather than reinscribe it.

This paper does not suggest that all lesbians should strive to make their personal advertisements and lives identical to the personal advertisements and lives of gay men with respect to sex. Neither does it suggest that all lesbians should engage in butch/femme or s/m sex. Nor does it suggest that lesbians need to rush out and buy dildos or harnesses, lipsticks or mini-skirts, erotic literature or sex toys. Rather, it makes a plea for sexual creativity. Talking and fantasizing about sex is an improvisational activity, one that calls for mutual awareness and willingness to experiment. Ideally, talking and fantasizing about sex is a path to greater sexual autonomy. Just as painters discover that they need not paint in one given way, but can experiment with styles, talking and fantasizing about sex encourages lesbians to see themselves as not confined to one form of sex, but able to both borrow from and question different styles of desire–sexual renegades at last.

REFERENCES

de Lauretis, Teresa. *The Practice of Love*. Indianapolis: Indiana UP, 1994.
Loulan, JoAnn. *The Lesbian Erotic Dance*. San Francisco: Spinsters, 1990.
Mohr, Richard. *Gay Ideas*. Boston: Beacon Press, 1992.
Pratt, Minnie Bruce. *S/HE*. Ithaca, New York: Firebrand Books, 1995.
Roy, Camille. "Speaking in Tongues." In *Sisters, Sexperts, Queers*, ed. A. Stein. New York: Penguin Books, 1993, 6-12.
Stein, Arlene, ed. *Sisters, Sexperts, Queers*. New York: Penguin Books, 1993.
Stein, Arlene. "The Year of the Lustful Lesbian." In *Sisters, Sexperts, Queers*, ed. A. Stein. New York: Penguin Books, 1993, 13-34.
Whorf, Benjamin. *Language, Though and Reality*. Cambridge, Boston: MIT Press, 1980.

Sex Radical Communities
and the Future of Sexual Ethics

Kathy Rudy

SUMMARY. Many urban-based gay male, lesbian, and mixed-gender sexually radical communities (such as leather and/or S/M groups) portray their interests in sexuality in terms of arousal and pleasure. The writings of many gays, lesbians, bisexuals, and queers involved in such communities suggest that sexual pleasure is based on individual preference, and that all sexual activities need only the consent of participating individuals to render those activities moral and good. Thus, as long as people consent, a wide variety of practices can be authorized in this system, such as non-monogamy, group sex, anonymous sex, domination, etc. In this paper, I will suggest that something much more radical is happening in these communities, that "individual preference" and "consent"–although present –are perhaps not the most interesting way to describe what is happening here. Rather, I will explore the possibility that these sex groups are in the process of providing for us a new kind of ethic based not on individuality, but rather based on community. *[Article copies available for a fee from The Haworth Document Delivery Service: 1-800-342-9678. E-mail address: getinfo@haworthpressinc.com]*

Kathy Rudy is Assistant Professor of Ethics and Women's Studies at Duke University. She holds a PhD in Theological Ethics, and is the author of *Sex and the Church: Gender, Homosexuality and the Transformation of Christian Ethics* and *Beyond Pro-Life and Pro-Choice: Moral Diversity in the Abortion Debate,* both on Beacon Press. She has written widely on issues of sexuality, reproduction, and medicine.

Address correspondence to: Kathy Rudy, Duke University, Durham, NC 27708.

[Haworth co-indexing entry note]: "Sex Radical Communities and the Future of Sexual Ethics." Rudy, Kathy. Co-published simultaneously in *Journal of Lesbian Studies* (The Haworth Press, Inc.) Vol. 3, No. 3, 1999, pp. 133-142; and: *Lesbian Sex Scandals: Sexual Practices, Identities, and Politics* (ed: Dawn Atkins) The Haworth Press, Inc., 1999, pp. 133-142; and: *Lesbian Sex Scandals: Sexual Practices, Identities, and Politics* (ed: Dawn Atkins) Harrington Park Press, an imprint of The Haworth Press, Inc., 1999, pp. 133-142. Single or multiple copies of this article are available for a fee from The Haworth Document Delivery Service [1-800-342-9678, 9:00 a.m. - 5:00 p.m. (EST). E-mail address: getinfo@haworthpressinc.com].

133

Community values are in fact just what we need, but they must be the values of our actual communities, not those of some abstract, universalized community that does not and cannot exist.

–Douglas Crimp (1990:19)

In an era where gay activism is increasingly synonymous with support for same-sex marriage, legalization of domestic partnerships, health and pension benefits for same-sex spouses, and gay couples who want their own children, it would benefit all of us to examine the ethical dimensions of sex. Why do we have sex? What principles can help us think about when sex is moral and good, and when it is oppressive, evil, or unhealthy? Thinking about the ethics of sex currently embedded in many historically gay, lesbian, bisexual, queer and transgendered practices, I suggest, might help us chart a course for a more radical politics in the future.

Sexual ethics is intended to lend clarity and insight into the reasons we engage in sexual activity. It has been a major component of the thinking involved in most religious institutions. (In this paper, I will be focusing only on the Christian tradition, as that is my training and background; other religious traditions have different codes of ethics which require separate study.) From the early admonitions of patristic fathers like Augustine and John Chrysostom, through medieval scholastics such as Aquinas, to the more recent proclamations of many Roman Catholics, many Christian thinkers have asserted that sex was moral only when it was both unitive and procreative. The word "unitivity" denotes intimacy, steadfastness, and one-fleshness. In the unitive nature of the sex act, two are made one; the boundaries of either individual are blurred–both literally and metaphorically–such that each individual becomes–at least momentarily–a part of something larger than him or herself. As Vincent Genovesi, S. J., describes it, "sexual intercourse is a sign of total, unreserved giving of self. [During sex], the individual's personality is lost in an interpenetration of the other self" (1987:154).

In traditional Christian thinking, however, the concept of unitivity alone was not enough to insure morality; thus, religious leaders also demanded that every act of sex be open to procreation. Under the influence of natural law, procreation came to be seen as the logical, objective, and dominant end of sex, the reason behind the function. Although not every sex act would lead to children, every sex act would be open to children as a way of insuring that the act was moral. Thus, as late as 1968, the Roman Catholic Church affirmed that "every matrimonial act must remain open to the transmission of life. To destroy even only partially the significance of intercourse and its ends is contradictory to the plan of God and to his will"

(Paragraph 14). Abortion, as well as all forms of birth control from condom use to the pill to coitus interruptus, are condemned by the teachings of the Roman Catholic magisterium. (In official Catholic teaching, the only form of conception control is the rhythm method whereby a couple abstains from sex during the fertile periods of the woman's ovulation cycle. The magisterium allows this intervention because, in their thinking, it is not a sexual activity which intentionally disrupts conception, but is rather the lack of sexual activity altogether.) For Catholics then, sex is good when it is both unitive and procreative, when man and woman are spiritually united in the act and when that act is open to the conception of children. Forms of sex which do not meet both of these criteria are outlawed.

Other ethical formulations have rejected the rule of procreativity, viewing sexual activity as important in and of itself without associating it with biological reproduction. For a variety of reasons (including the burden of large families and the oppression of women forced to bear and raise sometimes a dozen or more children), most Protestants in America eschew the ethic of procreativity for the more flexible notion of complementarity. Complementarity is the idea that men and women possess different natures, which are designed by God to complement each other, especially within the act of sex. For a man and a woman who love each other and seek to unite themselves, sex functions to fulfill God's theological design by incorporating these two differing, incomplete pieces into one, whole being. As Gareth Moore describes it:

> If a man and a woman are complementary, they go well together. Together they form a pleasing or appropriate whole, and it is that larger whole that is incomplete without one of the partners. It is like strawberries and cream. There are those who think that strawberries and cream are complementary. Because of their respective qualities they go well together, enhancing each other and forming a satisfying whole, the cream offsetting the sharpness of the strawberries and these in turn cutting the bland fattiness of the cream. Cream without strawberries or something similar is hardly to be contemplated, and when strawberries are served without cream, there is something missing. The strawberries, nice as they are alone, lack something. But it is not that the strawberries are incomplete, lack part of themselves. They lack or need something else, cream. Without the cream, it is not the fruit that is incomplete, but the dish . . . To say that men and women are complementary is to say that together they form a whole. (Moore, 1992:118-119)

Although the ethic of complementarity is designed to free the heterosexual couple from unwanted procreation, the problems that accompany complementarity are manifold. Complementarity covertly suggests that single, celibate, or uncoupled individuals are less than complete, and overtly suggests that homosexuals are unnatural and distorted. That is, if God designed men and women each to hold unique characteristics, certainly homosexual relationships must have a surplus of some characteristics and a deficiency of others.

While the church's teachings on matters of sex may not be the final authority, I want to suggest that these traditions function to normalize both heterosexuality and monogamy for most Americans today. Consequently, when gays and lesbians want to assimilate into dominant culture, we learn to do so largely by mimicking heterosexual relational structures. Our allegiances and commitments must belong not to any larger community but to our partner and nuclear family. We are encouraged to participate in the American dream by buying a house and living together, i.e., to separate ourselves from larger kinship systems. While living in our nuclear units, we will necessarily buy and use more than we would if we were part of a larger support community; we are urged, in short, to be good consumers. If consumption fails to keep us entertained, we are prodded to reproduce like heterosexuals, i.e., to "have" our "own" biological children through new reproductive technologies. Gay people today have become experts at impersonating straight nuclear families; the only thing that's different is that one of us is the wrong gender.

In resistance to these dictates, many progressive communities organize their sexual and social lives very differently. Urban-based gay male, lesbian, and mixed-gender sexually radical communities (such as leather and/or S/M groups) portray their interests in sexuality in terms of arousal and pleasure. These activities, often described as "anonymous," "promiscuous," or "non-relational" sex, have been widely criticized as dangerous, immature, or immoral. They are seen as the product of a particular kind of flawed psychology which is driven by a base and insatiable sexual desire and which consequently cannot commit to "mature sexuality," i.e., to monogamous relationship. I suggest to the contrary that many radical sex communities are comprised not of people who have failed to meet the "universal" standard of exclusive relationship, but rather of people who have organized their sexual-social lives on a different model, a model that is fundamentally communal. In many of these worlds, allegiance to the entire community is often more vital and meaningful than any particular coupling within that community; the attitudes generated by these practices can help shed light on new ways to think about progressive politics.

In America today, even in the age of AIDS, dozens of young people leave the small towns and heartlands every day and make their way to urban centers because they have come to believe that a community awaits them there. Sometimes they come only after reading about Castro Street in a magazine they once found left in a bathroom; sometimes they come after seeing a Primetime segment on Northhampton as the lesbian capital of the country; sometimes they come having memorized the entire map of New York City, knowing where every gay bar is on that map. Often they are driven by a desire to find a world where they will be accepted and honored, where they can belong without hiding a part of themselves. When they get there, they may well find a community of gays, lesbians, bisexuals, transgendered, and queer people who will remember what it is like to be young and alone and scared and broke. They will find others who believe, as Paul Monette writes it, that "it's a kind of duty to the tribe to take care of [these kids] and make it all less frightening" (1992:274). The fortunate ones will be initiated into the social fabric of that community not only through sex, but through crash courses in taste and style. There they will learn to renarrate their lives in the frame of queerness, to see themselves as always having belonged. They will stake out emotional territory inside the lives of others, and feel responsible even for those friends with whom they have not shared sex, for they recognize in this community that each is part of the other.

The many works of fiction, memoir and academic study stemming from and/or commenting on gay urban and radical sex cultures often feature a scene in which, for example, a young person finds his or her first sex in a bathroom, bar, or sex club and emerges from that space changed for the better. Celeste West's work on polyfidelity, for example, is filled with examples where lesbians connect with other lesbians for sex, companionship, and adventures of all kinds. As she imagines, "What if extra lovers were considered harmless fun, not framed as threatening? What if your lover having many lovers added to your presence? Cultivating the presence of new worlds alongside this one means an enlargement of life" (1996:11). Pat Califia expresses her anti-monogamy position even more forcefully: "I don't want to go back to living an economy of scarcity, clinging to one woman as if she were the only lesbian on earth" (1994:204). She encourages us to think critically–as gay people–outside the margins of marriage and monogamy. Works by men indicate similar realities; as Steven Seidman indicates,

> casual sex [is] viewed as a primary community building force in gay life. Through casual sex, gay men were said to experience heightened feelings of brotherhood and male solidarity . . . Barriers of age,

class, education and sometimes race were said to be weakened as individuals circulated in this system of sexual exchange; competition and rivalry between men might give ways to bonds of affection and kinship. (1991:186)

Though not all gay, lesbian, queer, or sex radical communities operate in this utopic fashion, in some, each sexual encounter shores up membership in the community and each person's participation makes the community she finds stronger for others. Although she may not know the names of each of her sex partners, each encounter resignifies her belonging. And although no two members of the community make steadfast promises to any one person in the community, each in his or her own way promises to remain part of this world. Intimacy and faithfulness in sex are played out on the community rather than individual level.

These cultures often challenge racial or class prejudices. As Frank Browning put it, "[t]he parks and the bathhouses have been places of freedom and fraternity . . . places where the cares and duties of the day dissolved, where barriers of class and education might temporarily evaporate" (1993:80-81). There is a sense in which the men in the parks and bathrooms, as well as lesbians in the growing number of women-only sex clubs in places like New York and San Francisco, have no separate identity, no history, no background except that of belonging to this community. Everything else about them, where they come from, what they do, is eclipsed by their identity as queer. These communities function and grow even in the AIDS crisis. The virus threatens each and every person; everyone who goes to a bar or "clit club" party or backroom to share sex—whether male or female, gay or straight—is vulnerable. And yet they continue to go. They leave behind high school diplomas, families who love them, college educations, chances of advancement, all to be part of this world. AIDS hasn't stopped these communities; indeed, it has only made them stronger.

I suggest that what happens in many of these cultures is not anonymous, promiscuous, or non-relational sex, but "communal." Sex in these worlds is not anonymous because that would mean that the partner is somehow unknown, and as one gay male friend of mine put it, "Even though I may not know his name, I know what music he listens to, what food he likes, where he vacations. His name is incidental. He's part of our world, that's all I need to know." Similarly, sex in these enclaves is far from promiscuous or indiscriminate because partners are chosen precisely because they belong inside that community, and because they show physical signs (such as taste in clothes, food, music, etc.) of participating in that world. Finally, sex in these communities is completely relational in that it functions as a way of inscribing members into an identity larger than oneself.

If you examine the writings of many gays, lesbians, bisexuals, and queers involved in these communities, most suggest that sexual pleasure is based on individual preference, and that all sexual activities need only the consent of participating individuals to render those activities acceptable. As long as people give consent and practice self-determination, they suggest, anything is okay. Partly as a result of the fact that sex radicals have repeatedly been told that they are abnormal and unethical, many are opposed to any kind of inquiry which tries to distinguish good sex from bad. Because "queerness" in the pejorative sense has always been defined by its negative relation to a particular moral code, many sex radicals assert that it is time to eliminate the barriers presented by all moral codes. As Gayle Rubin articulates it,

> Most of the discourses on sex, be they religious, psychiatric, popular, or political, delimit a very small portion of human sexual capacity as sanctifiable, safe, healthy, mature, legal, or politically correct. [A] 'line' distinguishes these from all other erotic behaviors, which are understood to be the work of the devil, dangerous, psychopathical, infantile, or politically reprehensible . . . we should [instead] judge sexual acts by the way partners treat one another, the level of mutual consideration, the presence or absence of coercion, and the quantity and quality of the pleasures they provide. Whether sex acts are gay or straight, coupled or in groups, naked or in underwear, commercial or free, with or without video, should not be an ethical concern. (1984:282-283)

In essence, sex radicals hope to make a place for alternative sexual expression that is completely free of the confining strictures of ethics. In resisting value judgments of what counts as good and bad sex, and in resting entirely on ideas such as self-determination, sex radicals invoke criteria of consent in order to establish a coherent category of protected sexually explicit materials and acts. What makes sex acceptable, in their view, has nothing to do with procreation, complementarity, or unitivity, but is related only to what we consent to.

However, mechanisms like consent and self-determination can be critiqued from many perspectives. A sole reliance on consent, for example, eventually leads to the reemergence of the liberal subject. In light of Marxism, feminism, and post-structuralism, I suggest that concepts like consent and self-determination are suspect. From a feminist point of view, for example, many women have so thoroughly absorbed the male gender codes that they have no idea what they really want, but have learned to want only what pleases men. As many feminist theorists have demonstrated, consent and coercion are not mutually exclusive absolutes but are usually encoded to varying degrees within the same system. Post-structuralist thinkers drive this critique even deeper. From their perspective, there is no subject present who really wants something, as we are all products of what we learn and where we identify. Post-structuralism disputes the idea that we can move beyond or beneath these constructed desires into a more genuine or true domain, because we are all social products of one discourse or another. It teaches us that individual choice always occurs in a context of constraint, stemming from processes which place definite limits on an individual's ability to exercise choice. What, then, does consent look like in light of these theories that draw our attention to the limitations of our own free-will?

Resting sexual practices on the ideas of consent and self-determination does not address the question of who gets to use them and when. Can a one-day-old baby give consent in any meaningful way? Can a person in a coma? Indeed, the NAMBLA controversy was not arguing over whether sex with very small children is right or wrong but rather whether age of consent should be fixed or flexible. One side of the NAMBLA debate argued for arbitrary state regulations (similar to voting age); the other suggested that sexual desire transcends such artificial boundaries. This problem arises because there is no completely logical, self-evident place to fix the idea of consent. Rather, it must be socially assigned, decreeing a given individual as a whole person who can and should think independently. It is ironic, then, that a person must be deemed to have an isolated, independent identity and will (and thus be able to give consent) in order to participate in an act which will unify him or her with another.

I also suggest that in our liberal system, the freedom to give consent is only granted to those who agree–first and foremost–to get along with others, to those who agree *not* to make waves for others, to those who keep their opinions and diversities confined to private spaces. Within this system, every person is forced to adopt an ironic relationship to those beliefs and practices that form and sustain her and must have no public commitment deeper than the project of peaceable living. Within such an ideology, queers and sex radicals are granted tolerance only when their practices are confined, for the most part, to private spaces (or to urban subcultures where queerness is the norm). The very mechanism that grants them this so-called freedom to engage in alternative sex practices in private denies them any meaningful public identity as a sex radical. Consent is thus an uneasy foundation for the practices and identities which sustain these cultures.

Rather than view these activities through the lens of consent, I suggest that what lends credibility and value to the acts, practices, beliefs, and identities circulating in sex radical cultures is the fact that they make sense to and within particular local communities. That is, I want to suggest that something much more disruptive is happening in these communities, that consent and self-determination—although present—are perhaps not the most interesting ways to describe what is happening here. These sex groups are in the process of providing us with a new kind of ethic based not on individuality, but rather on community.

In these sex radical cultures, sexual activities function as both initiations into community and as concrete practices that bind an entire culture together. Sex radical communities define for themselves what good sex is and how it should function; it is the community itself which serves as the foundation for determining good from bad, right from wrong. Who is in, who is out, what kinds of activities bring pleasure, what kinds are thought to be out of style, these and many other questions are worked out on a local, contingent level. Moreover, in these acts, any one person (often either male or female) can stand in for any other. The signifying factor is not a person's own unique identity, but rather the identity of group membership. And in each of these communities, when members are in need of care, housing, resources, etc., the entire community often responds, operating under the implicit assumption that each is responsible for the other. Rather than abstract dictums like procreation, complementarity, or consent, gays, lesbians, and queers of all sorts work out the ethics of their lives together on a day by day, practice by practice basis. The model of subjectivity that follows from these non-conventional sex practices, I argue, can help us form a new base of resistance for both sexual ethics and radical politics.

If the task of sexual ethics is to think about what makes sex good or bad, this communally based way of determining such value can help us think about what sexual ethics ought to look like after the fragmentation of the unified, autonomous subject. Not only is it the case that the sex radical communities decide together what counts as good and bad, they practice these activities with each other in ways that transcend individual identity and monogamy. They are functioning, it seems to me, as a participatory democracy that stands as a model for the postmodern. No longer defined by eighteenth-century notions of individuality, the sex radicals function as a model for a new subjectivity, radically intertwined, united, and interdependent, not with one other individual, but with an entire concrete, local community.

Sex radical communities, in short, can help us see how we can oppose oppressive frameworks with locally-based communities. The right's family values campaign has gained ground by promoting an idealized view of the family as America's salvation. In their focus on the family, conservative Christians appeal to those Americans who feel isolated and detached from meaningful senses of kinship and community. The family provides contemporary conservative Americans with a tool for overcoming the crippling and lonely effects of individuality. I suggest that gay and lesbian activists also need to challenge the value of the self-contained, isolated human subject by interpreting what happens in sex radical cultures as a function of community, not autonomous consent. Sex radical cultures stand as a model for all progressive Americans, testifying to the importance of belonging to a worthwhile cooperative as a way of making meaning in life.

REFERENCES:

Browning, Frank, *The Culture of Desire: Paradox and Perversity in Gay Lives Today.* New York: Crown Publishers, 1993.

Califia, Pat, *Public Sex: The Culture of Radical Sex.* Pittsburgh: Cleis Press, 1994.

Crimp, Douglas. *AIDS: Demographics.* Seattle: Bay Press, 1990.

Genovesi, Vincent J., S. J., *In Pursuit of Love: Catholic Morality and Human Sexuality.* Collegeville, Minnesota: The Liturgical Press, 1987.

Humanae Vitae. July 29, 1968.

Monette, Paul, *Becoming a Man: Half a Life Story.* San Francisco, Harper, 1992.

Moore, Gareth, O.P., *The Body in Context: Sex and Catholicism.* London: SCM Press, 1992.

Rubin, Gayle, "Thinking Sex: Notes for a Radical Theory of the Politics of Sexuality," in *Pleasure and Danger: Exploring Female Sexuality.* Carol Vance, ed., New York: Routledge, 1984, 267-319.

Seidman, Steven, *Romantic Longings: Love in America, 1830-1980.* New York: Routledge, 1991.

West, Celeste, *Lesbian Polyfidelity.* San Francisco: Booklegger Press, 1996.

Index

Page references with *n* followed by a number indicate endnotes, e.g., 80*n*2 refers to note 2 on page 80.

Abelove, Henry, 14
activism
    impact of queer theory on lesbian,
        16-17
    link with collective identity,
        12-13,17
ACT UP, 13,17
Adams, Parveen, 68-69
The Advocate, 29
African-American women, sexuality,
    18
Against Sadomasochism (Linden,
    Pagano, Russell and Star),
    48-50
AIDS
    lesbians and, 95
    radical sexual communities and,
        138
AIDS activism
    for female subcultures, 94
    queer movement and, 5,13,90
    shared values of, 100
*AIDS TV: Identity, Community and
    Alternative Video* (Juhasz),
    94
Anzaldúa, Gloria, 46
Aotearoa/New Zealand, lesbianism
    in, 104-106
Ashton, Charlotte, 120-121
assimilation
    differences devalued by, 5
    effect of, 4
    lesbian feminism movement
        towards, 89
    minority model, 3-4,8

"The Authenticating Goldfish:
    Reviewing Film and Video
    in the Nineties" (Rich), 93
Aviva (lesbian-identified bisexual),
    41-43
Awekotuku, Ngahuia Te, 105

Babe Bean, 75-76
Bad Attitude, 119
Bannon, Ann, 86
Barale, Michele, 14
Bataille, Georges, 62-68,70-71
bdsm (sexual practices). *See*
    sadomasochism; sexual
    practices
Beebo Brinker (Bannon), 86
Benjamin, Jessica, 68
Bersani, Leo, 90
binary logic and structure
    lesbian identity constructed
        through, 22-25
    queering by stone butch/femme
        couples, 88
biphobia, 35-36,40,42
"birth bodies," 7,73,78
bisexuality
    lesbian reaction to, 36-38
    political opposition to, 4-5,15
    queer theory and, 18
    seen as a threat, 47,107
black. *See* African-American; people
    of color
"Black (w)holes and the Geometry
    of Black Female Sexuality"
    (Hammonds), 18

   143

Haworth
DOCUMENT DELIVERY
SERVICE

This valuable service provides a single-article order form for any article from a Haworth journal.

- *Time Saving:* No running around from library to library to find a specific article.
- *Cost Effective:* All costs are kept down to a minimum.
- *Fast Delivery:* Choose from several options, including same-day FAX.
- *No Copyright Hassles:* You will be supplied by the original publisher.
- *Easy Payment:* Choose from several easy payment methods.

Open Accounts Welcome for . . .
- Library Interlibrary Loan Departments
- Library Network/Consortia Wishing to Provide Single-Article Services
- Indexing/Abstracting Services with Single Article Provision Services
- Document Provision Brokers and Freelance Information Service Providers

---

MAIL or *FAX* THIS ENTIRE ORDER FORM TO:

Haworth Document Delivery Service
The Haworth Press, Inc.
10 Alice Street
Binghamton, NY 13904-1580

or FAX: 1-800-895-0582
or CALL: 1-800-429-6784
9am-5pm EST

PLEASE SEND ME PHOTOCOPIES OF THE FOLLOWING SINGLE ARTICLES:

1) Journal Title: _____

    Vol/Issue/Year:_____Starting & Ending Pages:_____

Article Title:_____

_____

2) Journal Title: _____

    Vol/Issue/Year:_____Starting & Ending Pages:_____

Article Title:_____

_____

3) Journal Title: _____

    Vol/Issue/Year:_____Starting & Ending Pages:_____

Article Title:_____

_____

4) Journal Title: _____

    Vol/Issue/Year:_____Starting & Ending Pages:_____

Article Title:_____

(See other side for Costs and Payment Information)

COSTS: Please figure your cost to order quality copies of an article.

1. Set-up charge per article: $8.00
   ($8.00 × number of separate articles)   _____

2. Photocopying charge for each article:
   1-10 pages: $1.00   _____

   11-19 pages: $3.00   _____

   20-29 pages: $5.00   _____

   30+ pages: $2.00/10 pages   _____

3. Flexicover (optional): $2.00/article   _____

4. Postage & Handling: US: $1.00 for the first article/
   $.50 each additional article   _____

   Federal Express: $25.00   _____

   Outside US: $2.00 for first article/
   $.50 each additional article   _____

5. Same-day FAX service: $.50 per page   _____

GRAND TOTAL: _____

METHOD OF PAYMENT: (please check one)

❏ Check enclosed   ❏ Please ship and bill. PO # _____
   (sorry we can ship and bill to bookstores only! All others must pre-pay)

❏ Charge to my credit card: ❏ Visa;   ❏ MasterCard;   ❏ Discover;
   ❏ American Express;

Account Number: _____ Expiration date: _____

Signature: ✗ _____

Name: _____ Institution: _____

Address: _____

_____

City: _____ State: _____ Zip: _____

Phone Number: _____ FAX Number: _____

MAIL or *FAX* THIS ENTIRE ORDER FORM TO:

Haworth Document Delivery Service   **or FAX:** 1-800-895-0582
The Haworth Press, Inc.   **or CALL:** 1-800-429-6784
10 Alice Street   (9am-5pm EST)
Binghamton, NY 13904-1580

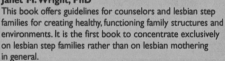